Essential Teachings of Maitreya

The Essential Nature of Phenomena

The Buddha Nature

The Middle Way

Translated with Introductions and Notes by

Dorje Jinpa

Pentarba Publications

Also by Dorje Jinpa

SENSA: The Lost Language of the Ancient Mysteries

A Synthesis of Alchemy: An Enquiry into the Secrets of Hermetic Philosophy

Essential Teachings of Maitreya: Three Complete Works

Secrets of the Heart

The Book of Hermes

The Coming Avatar

Gates to Infinity: A Commentary on the Agni Yoga Infinity Teachings

Available at pentarba.com

100 copies 2020

Sold online at pentarba.com

Om Muni Muni Smara Svaha[1]

With reverence and joy I bow
To Maitreya, the coming Buddha.
May the purity of His Teachings be maintained!
May they bring joy and cessation of suffering!

---

[1] This mantra, when sounded with heart-felt intent, is said to unite the devote with the heart of Maitreya.

Contents

Preface

Maitreya, the tenth degree Bodhisattva and future Buddha, is said to have miraculously appeared to Asanga after a twelve-year meditational retreat, transported him in consciousness to the Tushita Heavens where he gave him five Treasure Lineage teachings, three of which are translated here from the original Sanskrit. This miraculous event is confirmed by many worthy Tibetan scholars including Asanga himself, who wrote many commentaries based upon them, his brother Vasubandhu, who also gave many discourses based upon these teachings, and by two of Buddhism's greatest historians Buston (1290–1364) and Taranatha (1575-1634).

These teachings, along with their many commentaries, are the primary source works for the great Yogachara tradition in India and Tibet. This tradition recognizes two kinds of lineages, outer and inner. The outer lineage follows the unbroken line of teachings from teacher to disciples. The inner Treasure Lineage (*Tatnagotra*), illuminated by Maitreya, refers to the unbroken universal continuum of the Buddha Nature within all beings (*tathagatagotra*).

Each of the three teachings by Maitreya presented here clarifies the nature of reality from a different perspective. The first explores the fundamental nature of phenomena, the material universe, by examining the difference that exists between its appearance in form and its essential nature, which is hidden from view.

The second teaching explores the Buddha Nature, the pure seed of Buddhahood inherent, yet latent, within all beings, its gradual uncovering, and its eventual full flowering as the Dharmakaya, the fully awakened primordial awareness nature of a Buddha.

The third teaching, *The Middle Way*, illuminates the Buddha's teaching on emptiness, the non-dual nature of reality. It is in this teaching that the Yogachara tradition, which bases its doctrine, to a large extent, upon the teachings of Maitreya, and the Madhyamaka tradition, which primarily bases its doctrine upon the teachings of Nagarjuna, find common ground. The realization of emptiness, we are told, ultimately transcends both sides of the equation— nirvana and samsara, primordial mind and conceptual mind, the non-relative and relative, infinity and the finite, unity and diversity, etc.

> "It is neither real nor not real," says Maitreya.
> "Its essential nature is real.
> Its appearance in form is not.
> The nature of reality is beyond both of these.
> This is the middle way."

Due to the esoteric nature of these teachings they were written in a simple highly condensed *karika* form in which many of the necessary words were abbreviated, implied, or left out altogether. This was done, we are told, to protect those students who were not yet ready to receive and understand them correctly. Traditionally such esoteric teachings were explained by additional oral instruction and commentaries by a teacher who understood their meaning. The following translations are offered in an attempt to accurately clarify the teachings without the need for lengthy commentaries. Words and phrases contained in (parenthesis) represent that which is implied, but not actually stated in the original text. For easy reading simply ignore them. Some headings have been added for the sake of clarity.

I have been guided in this endeavor by my Teacher and by the excellent commentaries on Maitreya's Treasure Lineage teachings given by Asanga, Vasubandhu, Hsuan-tsang, Dolpopa, Longchenpa, Mipham, Jamgon Kongtrul, and Kalu Rinpoche.

May the spiritual energy and merit that is sure to be generated by anyone who reads, contemplates, and attempts to apply these precious teachings in life be instrumental in the liberation of all beings from suffering.

Book One

The Essential Nature of Phenomena

Dharma Dharmata Vibhaga Karika:
A concise analysis in verse of the difference between the
appearance of phenomena and its essential nature.

Introduction to the Essential Nature of Phenomena

The following teaching by Maitreya contains instruction on how to transform the appearance of phenomena (*dharma*), which we all share in common, into an awareness of the essential nature of phenomena (*dharmata*), which is shared only by the great Buddhas and Bodhisattvas.

The Sanskrit term '*dharma*' in the title means 'phenomena,' a material or conceptual manifestation in form, as in the famous statement by the Blessed One, "All dharmas are empty of reality." The term arises from the root *dhri*, meaning 'to manifest.' It is also popularly used in Buddhism as an abbreviation for *Buddhadharma*, meaning a manifestation of Buddha's wisdom, though that is not how it is being used here. The term '*dharmata*' means the essential or true nature (*ta*) of phenomena (*dharma*), the reality behind its illusive appearance in form. '*Vibhaga*' means an analysis, and '*karika*' means a concise scripture written in verse.

The true nature of material or conceptual phenomena is not perceived, says Maitreya, because of our dualistic view, which sees the object of our perceptions as something separate from the observer. This habitual view, says Maitreya, is not only false, "it is the root cause of all our problems." The remedy for this false perception, he tells us, is the realization of the non-dual nature of reality, wherein all sense of separation between perceiver, perceived, and the act of perceiving has been eliminated. This is called '*dharmata*,' or '*dharmadhatu*,' the true nature of all life in samsara and nirvana.

The difference, as well as the non-difference, that exist between the appearance of phenomena and its essential nature is the primary theme of this work. It is first necessary, says Maitreya, to perceive the difference between the appearance of phenomena and its true nature before we can understand that from a higher perspective there is no difference between them at all. While this may seem like an unsolvable paradox it can, perhaps, be kept in perspective through an understanding of the indivisible nature of the 'two truths,' relative and non-relative. The Blessed One, throughout his teachings, skillfully blended together these two truths. In the *Diamond Sutra*, for example, he is quoted as saying how important it is that the Bhiksus work towards the liberation of all sentient beings, while in the same breath he states that there are no sentient beings to save. In another example from the *Great Perfection of Wisdom Sutra* Subhuti asked the Buddha about the signs and characteristics of a Bodhisattva. The Buddha answered by saying that all dharmas are empty of signs and characteristics. He then proceeded to list all the signs and characteristics of a Bodhisattva. Are these true contradictions or simply a skillful way of demonstrating the non-duality of the two truths, relative and non-relative?

> "Conceptual wisdom," says Maitreya, "leads to
> spiritual freedom.
> Non-conceptual wisdom *is* spiritual freedom."[1]

Through the relative truths of conceptual wisdom the disciples of the Buddha follow the Eight Fold Path that leads to the attainment of non-conceptual enlightenment.[2]

Mipham, in his commentary on the present text, addresses this question thus:

> The wisdom of the Buddha understands the reality
> of the two truths (relative and non-relative) to be
> pure, indivisible and of one taste.

In the following teaching, Maitreya gives concise meditation instructions that can be used to eliminate false dualistic perceptions. We are guided through four levels of meditation practice: Meditation upon an object, meditation without an object, meditation without a subject (without an observer), and finally in verse 47,

---
[1] *The Buddha Nature*, verse 3: 14
[2] See verse 10. below

By holding one's attention upon awareness itself without separating it into two [awareness watching awareness] one arrives at primordial wisdom.

The Essential Nature of Phenomena

Dharma Dharmata Vibhaga Karika:
A treatise (*vibhaga*) in verse (*karika*) on the appearance of phenomena
(*dharma*) and its essential nature (*dharmata*).

The following (verses) contain a brief explanation of two (kinds of
perception):
The (false) perception of material and conceptual phenomena and
The (true perception) of the essential nature of phenomena.

The (false) perception of phenomena is samsara.
It is to be completely eliminated through correct understanding.

The (true) perception of the essential nature of phenomena is nirvana.
It is the cessation of suffering.
It (naturally) arises as the three vehicles of a Buddha.[1]
It is to be realized fully.

Due to (our) dualistic perception,

---

[1] The Dharmakaya, Sambhogakaya, and Nirmanakaya.

The world appears to be separate from the observer.   5

That which appears in this way is not real.

All dualistic relationships are unreal.

Being but concepts they exist only as concepts.

The dharmata,

The fundamental nature of phenomena,

Is real.

It contains no individual characteristics,

No separation between perceiver and perceived.

There is delusion because that which is not real appears (to the mind).

This delusion is the root cause of all our problems.

That which appears (in this way) is like an imaginary elephant.

It prevents that which is real from being perceived.

If this were not true then it would be unreasonable to pursue the path to

spiritual freedom,

Which leads from the delusion of psychic impurities

To a transformation (of the consciousness).

These two,

(Phenomena and its essential nature),

Are not the same.

Yet neither are they different. [1]

---

[1] Spiritual paradoxes, such as this, are based upon the fact that we are approaching a single truth from two perspectives, relative and non-relative. From a relative perspective of

A distinction must be made between what is real and what is not real.
And yet (from a higher perspective) there is no difference between them
at all.   10

To clarify (the nature of phenomena) six points are given:
1. Its characteristics
2. Its reason (for appearing)
3. The fact that it different and not different
4. The common ground (of incorrect perception)
5. The uncommon ground (of correct perception)
6. The realization that the fundamental nature of reality
Is beyond the appearances created by the duality of perceiver and
perceived.
This is the best way (to approach the subject).

(The first three), its characteristics, its reason (for appearing)
And the fact that it is both difference and not different,
Have been briefly covered (above).

In all cases involving cyclic existence (*samsara*)
The basis of perception lies in (two) aspects:
1. That which is within us
2. (That which is external), our bodies

The basis of experience common to all is the perception of our bodies.

---

conceptual thinking they are different; but from the higher perspective of non-conceptual
wisdom they are not.

The basis of experience not common to all is that which is within us.

Perceptions common to all arise because of the mutual interaction.

This includes the birth of the body,

Its characteristics,

Its positive or negative qualities,

And it's nurturing and disciplining.

That which appears to be external is perceived in common (with others).

It (falsely) appears to be distinct form awareness itself.[1]

Experience not shared with others pertains to awareness.

Is (your) mind perceived by others?   15

Those whose minds are agitated will not perceive the Mind itself.

Those not abiding in meditative quiescence perceive (only) their own thoughts.

Those abiding in (meditative) quiescence perceive the true nature of Mind.

Primordial awareness is perceived during absorption in samadhi.[2]

If that which we perceive (outside of us) is not true,

Then that which perceives (an outside world) is also not true.

From this we can understand the need to obtain liberation

From the dual appearance of perceiver and perceived.

---

[1] "I do not admit the existence of an external world," states the Buddha in the *Lankavatara Sutra*. "I teach that the 'three worlds' [of samsara] exist only in the mind. I do not teach the appearance of multiplicity."

[2] Samadhi is a state of profound meditative absorption where the separation of subject and object has been eliminated.

The non-duality of perceiver and perceived is,
And has always been, the reality.

Instruction on the supreme path to the essential nature of reality
Is clarified through six aspects:
1. Its defining characteristics
2. Its unchanging basis
3. Its verification
4. The realization
5. Meditation
6. A total absorption in reality

Its defining characteristics have been briefly given (above).   20
The basis arises from the supreme teachings of the Buddha.
Verification is obtained through a transformation of the consciousness
According to the Buddha's instructions.

The realization of primordial awareness is attained through
Correct view
Continual mindfulness
Removing all the psychic impurities that prevent enlightenment
And through a consciousness focused in meditation.

Final transformation,
Union with unchanging reality,
Arises when these impurities are removed.

The following ten considerations

Provide an excellent introduction into the nature of this transformation:

1. The fundamental nature (of sentiency)

2. Aspects (of the transformation process)

3. The individuals involved

4. The special characteristics

5. Its (necessary) prerequisites

6. The foundation (upon which enlightenment is built)

7. Refinement of consciousness

8. The application (of the meditation techniques)

9. Its disadvantages

10. Its advantages   25

The nature (of sentiency) is both pure and stained.

It is pure in its primordial condition.

It is stained when it appears in form.

The sutras (of the Buddha) transform the (false) appearances

That we share in common with others

Into an awareness of reality that is not shared in common.

Those who experience this transformation are

Buddhas, bodhisattvas, shravakas and pratyekabuddhas.

The greatest transformation is attained by Buddhas and Bodhisattvas

Because their realization arises as the three vehicles,

Nirmanakaya, Sambhogakaya and the Dharmakaya,

Each of which is of progressively greater value.

The prerequisites (necessary for the transformation) include:

Prayer

A concentrated study of the Mahayana Teachings

And an understanding of the Bhumis or levels of enlightenment.   30

The basis (for the transformation of the consciousness) is non-conceptual

wisdom.

It is built upon six (foundation stones):

1. A clear focused direction

2. Non-attachment

3. Taming the mind through the practice (of meditation)

4. (Understanding) the defining characteristics

5. (Understanding) the benefits (of transformation)

6. Full realization

The first of these, a clear focused direction,

Is attained by the following four aspects:

1. The Mahayana teachings

2. A strong commitment (to follow these teachings)

3. A strong conviction (in its truth)

4. Full application of its instructions

The second (foundation stone) is non-attachment.

There are four kinds of attachment that must be eliminated:

1. The (course) attachment to unfavorable characteristics

2. The (medium) attachment to the antidotes (the practice itself)

3. The (subtle) attachment to the experience of realization

4. The (very subtle) attachment to union with reality

These (attachments) should be given up in the following stages:

(First) the course (attachments to unfavorable characteristics in oneself),

(Then) the medium (attachment to one's practice),

And (finally) the subtle (attachment to the realization of and absorption in reality).

(These attachments are called) samskaras,[1]

They have existed (in the mind-stream) for a long time.

All attachments must be eliminated.

(The third foundation stone), is the practice of wisdom meditation.

It consists of four parts or stages:

1. Steady (one pointed) awareness upon an object

2. Steady awareness without an object

3. Steady awareness without a subject (without an observer)

4. Steady awareness (itself) without a subject or an object.   35

(The forth foundation stone of primordial wisdom),

Its defining characteristics,

Can be understood from three perspectives:

---

[1] Samskaras are habitual tendencies created by karma.

1. As the indivisible fundamental nature of reality

2. As the absence of dualistic appearances

3. And as that which is beyond concepts

(The first) abides in the fundamental nature of reality.

(The second) is primordial wisdom as described in the sutras;

As the absence of appearances,

"Without forms and vehicles,

Without an individual perspective,

Without worlds and principles,

And arising as illusions in the space in front."

(And finally the third aspect)

It cannot be defined as it is beyond all conceptual analysis.

(The fifth foundation stone of primordial wisdom)

Arises as the attainment of four benefits:

1. The dharmakaya

2. Unsurpassable bliss,

3. The power to obtain direct knowledge

4. The power to teach

From these four (benefits) arise:

1. An understanding of the antidote (to delusion and suffering)

2. (An understanding of the) characteristics (of correct transcendence)

3. As the signs of accomplishment

4. As the fruit (enlightenment)   40

The antidote is non-conceptual primordial awareness.

It removes the five delusions:

1. The delusion of outer appearances

2. The delusion of separate selves

3. The delusion of change (or time)

4. The delusion of duality

5. The delusion of doubt

Primordial awareness has five characteristics:

1. It is without thought

2. It is the essential nature of (ordinary) awareness

3. It is silent and still

4. It is without preconceptions

5. It is without parts or divisions

The five signs of its attainment include an awareness that is:

1. All-inclusive

2. Free of conceptual divisions

3. Essentially unchanging

4. Unborn yet always present

5. Unexcelled

The last (foundation stone of primordial wisdom)

Consists of five beneficial effects:

1. Unsurpassed joy

2. The elimination of all outside conditioning,[1]

Conceptual divisions,

And emotional impurities

3. The total freedom of the spiritual world (*dharmadhatu*).

4. Access to any information

5. The power to transmit the realizations of truth to spiritually mature

sentient beings

Bodhisattvas for whom the essential nature of reality is still unknown,

And in whom the cause of dualistic appearance still remains,

Follow the instructions that develop the mind.

In this way they pass through the gate of non-duality,

And reach the shore of pure primordial awareness.   45

When phenomena appears (to be distinct from the observer)

The essential nature of reality is not perceived.

When (dualistic) appearance disappears the truth is realized.

By properly developing the mind in non-dual perception

The bodhisattvas pass through the gate of non-duality.

By focusing one's attention upon awareness itself

Without separating it into two (awareness watching awareness)

One arrives at primordial wisdom.

---

[1] "The Bodhisattvas, though they continuously work to benefit the world, nevertheless remain unaffected by it. Just as a lotus flower grows in (muddy) water and yet is not polluted by it, so the great Bodhisattvas live in the world and yet are not polluted by it." *The Buddha Nature,* verse 1-71

This is the meaning (of the previous meditation instructions),

To meditate without an object,

Without a subject,

And without subject and object (together).

This is (now) precisely defined.

By progressing through these four stages of meditation

One attains four levels (of realization).

The first stage, (meditation with an object)

Is (called) Informed Commitment.

Through unwavering resolve,

Using the teaching (itself) as the object of meditation,

Verification (of it) is obtained through firsthand experience.   50

The second stage (meditation without an object)

Is called Encountering the True.

It consists of the transformation of the impure levels (of consciousness)

into the pure.

The third stage,

(Meditation without a subject)

Is called The Great Recollection.

It consists of the complete transformation (of ones skandas)

Into the three pure (vehicles of a Buddha).

The final perfection is called, Absorption into the Essence.
It is the spontaneous expression of primordial wisdom
As the ceaseless activity of a Buddha.

The four disadvantages of failing to make the transformations are:
1. Not being able to stop (thoughts) from arising at their source
2. Not understanding the basis of the path
3. Not being able to affirm the truth of nirvana (to others)
4. Not being able to demonstrate the manifestation of the three vehicles
of the Buddha

The four advantages are the reverse of these:
(1. The ability to stop impure thoughts from arising
2. The ability to understand the basis of the path
3. The ability to affirm the goal of nirvana from experience
4. The ability to demonstrate the nature of the three vehicles)

To illustrate how unreal (dualistic) appearances appear (to the mind),
the Mahayana teachings have likened them to dreams, mirages, and
illusions.
To illustrate the nature of a totally transformed awareness,
It has been compared to (infinite) space,
And to the radiance of gold reflected in water, etc.   55

Book Two

The Buddha Nature

Introduction to the Buddha Nature

> Oh Sariputra, non-relative reality (*paramarthasatya*)
> is not different from the essential nature of
> beings (*attvadhatu*). The essential nature of beings
> is not different from the seed of buddhahood
> (*tathagatagarbha*). The seed of buddhahood is not
> different from the dharmakaya, the primordial
> awareness nature of a Buddha.
>
> — *Dharanisvara Sutra*

The following teaching by Maitreya is essentially a commentary on the third and final round of the sutra teachings given by the Blessed One prior to his passing into the highest nirvana. In this round the Buddha gave teachings on the Buddha-nature, the pure seed of buddhahood eternally present within all beings. This third round, says Maitreya, "represents the Buddha's greatest teachings." Longchenpa, an Arhat of the Great Perfection lineage of Tibet, writes:

The third turning of the wheel of the dharma contains the Buddha's definitive meaning. It shows the absolute, the great secret of all the Buddhas. In it we find an explanation of the true nature of the mind, which is the same as the Buddha-nature eternally present in all beings.

Jamgon Kongtrul (1813-1900), in the introduction to his commentary on this text by Maitreya, states:

> The Buddha gave teachings on many levels according to the faculties of his listeners. The Buddha-nature sutras of the third round are of the highest level.... The teachings on the heart essence of a Buddha are supreme over all the subjects taught by the perfect and complete Buddha. They are the highest summit of the Mahayana teachings.

In the *Nirvana Sutra*[1] the Buddha states that his teaching on the Buddha-nature is 'the absolute and final culmination of my teaching.'

In his first cycle of teachings the Blessed One taught the fundamental formula for the liberation of human beings from suffering:

1. Humanity is suffering.
2. The primary cause of this suffering is desire arising from ignorance.

---

[1] *Mahayana Mahaparinirvana Sutra*

3. The cessation of suffering, therefore, is attained through wisdom.

4. Wisdom is attained by following the eightfold spiritual path.

In his second cycle of teachings the Blessed One taught that all dharmas, all material and conceptual phenomena including the idea of a self (separate identity), ultimately lack reality. In his third series of teachings he taught that while beings and phenomena lack any independent life, characteristics, or identity of their own, the true nature and cause of phenomena and beings is in fact pure, unchanging and like space, is infinite, undivided and all-pervasive.

In the second series of teachings the Blessed One approached the nature of reality from the particular to the universal through the well known process of negation—not form, not many, not a duality, not conceptual, not divisible into parts, and not the sum total of all parts. In the third round of teachings he approached the same reality but in the reverse order, from the universal to the particular through the affirmation of the essential nature of reality within all beings (*dharmakaya*) and within all phenomena (*dharmata*). As reality (*tathata*) is beyond the duality of opposites there is no real contradiction between the negation of emptiness (second round) and the affirmation of all-inclusiveness (third round).

It is not a positive for it denies duality.

It is not a negative for it affirms reality.

In the second round the Buddha states that all things are insubstantial, like a dream, like reflections in a mirror. In the third round he gave teachings on the source, cause, and fundamental nature of these reflections. He taught that what remains after all the impurities and illusions are removed is the pure wisdom nature of a Buddha, the essential unchanging basis of all experience in samsara and nirvana.

The great Nagarjuna explains the three turnings of the wheel of Buddhadharma as three ways of approaching the *one* unchanging truth. In the first round of teachings, he says, the Lord Buddha taught about the self. Next he taught about the not-self. And finally in the third turning of the wheel he gave teachings to resolve the seeming contradiction that arose from the first two.

Gyurmed Tshewang Chogtrub states:

In the second turning of the wheel the Buddha elaborately taught the inconceivable nature through the ways of non-conceptualization…. In the third turning of the wheel he disclosed the presence of the [Buddha]-Essence, but he didn't disclose the definite path that realizes that essence. Dzogchen, without contradicting them, embodies the ultimate vision of both Great Chariots; (a) the vision of the second turning of the wheel elucidated by Nagarjuna…. and (b) the vision of the third turning of the wheel elucidated by Maitreya, the Great Regent, and the Noble Asanga and his brother (Vasubandhu).[1]

Padmasambhava, the immortal Bodhisattva who, even in this degenerate age, is said to be still actively working for the liberation of all beings, lists a few of the names by which the Buddha-nature is known.

> It is called the *Heart Essence of a Buddha*, because it is the heart of emptiness. It is called the *Perfection of Wisdom* because to realize its nature is to transcend everything. It is called the *Mahamudra* because it is beyond the intellect. It is called the *Alayavijnana* (the basis of consciousness) because it is the root of everything, the bliss of nirvana as well as the sorrow of samsara. And when confined within the mundane (human) sphere, though this awareness is ever present, lucid and clear, it is called *ordinary awareness*. No matter what name we use the meaning is this ever present awareness.[2]

In this teaching by Maitreya several Sanskrit terms are given to represent the Buddha-nature including *dhatu*, which is an abbreviation of *buddhadhatu* meaning the essential element of a Buddha. In its latent unrealized condition it is called the *Tathagata-garbha*, the seed (*garbha*) of a Buddha (*tathagata*). When the Buddha-nature is fully

---

[1] Quoted by Tulku Thondup in his illuminating treatise *The Practice of Dzogchen*, Snow Lion 2002.
[2] *Liberation Through Primordial Awareness (Rigpa Ngosprod Gcermthog Rangrol)*.

realized it is called the *dharmakaya*. In both cases, says Maitreya, whether hidden by psychic impurities or fully realized, it is:

> Eternally unchanging and pure, the true, undivided
> universal nature of the mind, the supreme continuum of
> primordial awareness, the root, seed-essence, and fruit of
> unsurpassable enlightenment, the origin of all experiences
> in samsara and nirvana, and the essential nature and true
> identity of all beings.

Although these facts are clearly stated by Maitreya in the following teaching and by the Blessed One throughout many of his sutra teachings of the third round, there has in the past been some question among Buddhists as to whether the wisdom nature of a Buddha is ultimately real; or whether, like the appearance of phenomena, it too is an illusion, arising like a dream. The cause of this controversy is the seeming (but not actual as this teaching clearly demonstrates) contradiction between the teachings given by the Buddha during the second and third round.[1] Maitreya addresses and answers this question as follows:

---

[1] Teachings on the two perspectives of reality as given in the 2nd and 3rd round was given by the First Panchen Lama in his, *The Harmony of the Two Correct Views of Reality*, which forms a part of his *The Main Road of the Triumphant Ones*. It is further discussed by the Dalai Lama in his commentary on this work in *The Gelug/Kagyu Tradition of Mahamudra*, Snow Lion 1997, pages 234 – 239.

(Question) In the earlier teachings (of the second round) it is said that 'perceptions of the mind are unreal, being like clouds, like visions in a dream, like an illusion.' So how is it that the Lord declares here (in the third round) that 'the essential nature of a Buddha exists in all beings'? (Answer) The Buddha-nature is empty of all individual characteristics, conceptual divisions, and impurities. It is not empty of the highest. It is indivisible with it.

Maitreya continues:

If the spiritual nature of a Buddha did not exist there would be no impulse to be liberated from the suffering of samsara and no heartfelt attraction to nirvana. Samsara is full of suffering and is therefore impure. Nirvana is bliss and therefore has merit. Neither would exist without the Buddha-principle present in all beings.

To reconcile the seeming discrepancy between the teachings of the second and third round it became popular to regarded the sutra teachings of the third round as being less true than the second. For this reason the sutra teachings of the third turning of the wheel has been for the most part ignored. According to Maitreya the present text on the Buddha-nature was given in part to correct this mistake. The seeming contradiction is reconciled when it is realized that the fundamental nature of all beings, the *Buddhadhatu*, is not an individual essence but rather a universal principle.

Some Buddhists deny the reality of the Buddha-nature by saying that 'its nature is emptiness.' But emptiness (*shunyata*), we must remember, is not an absolute negation. In fact as Maitreya points out it negates only that which is unreal. The Sanskrit term 'shunyata' is a compound of 'shunya' meaning 'empty,' and the suffix 'ta' here meaning 'nature of.' Shunyata represents the essential nature of the negated appearance and not the negation itself. It certainly does not negate the reality of primordial wisdom. If it did it would it also negate the Buddha's teachings on nirvana. Thrangu Rinpoche in his commentary to Maitreya's *Distinguishing Dharma and Dharmata* states:

> Emptiness is not a voidness nor a mere nothingness, in
> which nothing whatsoever exists. Rather, it has the nature
> of luminous clarity, which is the basis for the Buddha's
> wisdom, the development of a Buddha's omniscience.[1]

From the perspective of the Maitreya's teachings, the empty nature of the Buddha-essence means that like space it cannot be divided into parts, individual characteristics, or conceptual divisions; it cannot be separated into perceiver, perceived, or the act of perception. It has no form, boundaries, or limits either in time or in space. Longchenpa writes:

---

[1] Sri Satguru Publications, 1999, translated by Jules Levinson, p. 46.

Even bodhisattvas of the tenth level (the highest) have only a partial understanding of the Buddha-nature. Only a Buddha understands it completely.

The truth of the Buddha-nature therefore cannot be classified as 'one of the Buddha's lesser truths' unless we can agree that *all* of the Buddha's Teachings are addressing the unchanging reality from a certain level or perspective simply because the absolute itself cannot be stated in words or given as a concept. "Whatever is taught," said the Buddha, "is a distortion of the truth, for the truth itself is beyond words."[1] Subhuti, at the moment of his enlightenment and in the presence of the Blessed One, is said to have proclaimed, "The Tathagata has nothing to teach."[2]

According to Maitreya the Buddha's paradoxical teachings on the empty, insubstantial nature of beings and phenomena and his teachings on the space-like fullness of the essential nature of all beings and phenomena are not opposed. They both *point to*, without defining, the same inexpressible fundamental nature of reality, which has no opposite. Maitreya, in his teaching on the *Essential Nature of Phenomena* given above, explains the difference in emphasis between these two approaches to the truth:

---

[1] *Lankavatara Sutra*
[2] *The Diamond Cutter Sutra*

To illustrate how unreal appearances arise, the Mahayana Teachings have likened them to dreams, mirages, etc. To illustrate the nature of a totally transformed awareness, it has been compared to space.[1]

Maitreya, closely following the Buddha's teachings as given in the third round, states that it is the delusions, conceptual divisions, and unnatural psychic impurities, that are unreal, and not the enlightened perceptions of a Buddha.

> The impurities of living beings are unnatural, without any reality, yet the essential nature of these impurities, though empty of material and conceptual reality, are nevertheless real.

The scriptural authority for this view can be found in a statement given by the Blessed One in his *Shrimaladevi Sutra*.

> The emptiness (*shunyata*) of the Buddha-nature (*tathagata-garbha*) can be understood in two ways. It is empty (*shunya*) of all psychic impurities, conceptual divisions, and limitations. It is not empty (*ashunya*) of the inconceivable qualities of a Buddha, which are as numerous as the sands of the Ganga; it is not empty of clear perception and spiritual freedom.

---

[1] Verse 55

It is not that the realization of Buddha-nature is somehow greater than the realization of emptiness, but rather that without realization of the Buddha-nature realization of emptiness is impossible.

The Buddha has many times warned us not to conceptualize the idea of emptiness as this would prevent realization. Maitreya's teaching of the *Middle Way*, which is to follow, proclaims:

> The conquerors have said that emptiness uproots all views. Those who have a (preconceived) view of emptiness will have no accomplishment.

Buddhism, then, should be approached as a path to enlightenment and not as a collection of dogmatic assertions as to the nature of reality. Emptiness, we are told, cannot be grasped by the conceptual mind. It must, therefore, be approached through a higher facility than the rational mind, through the primordial awareness nature of the Buddha, the heart essence of all the Buddhas. The very first level (*bhumi*) of enlightenment, says Maitreya, is the realization of innate purity of the Buddha-nature. Without the Seed of Buddhahood (*tathagatagarbha*) the Tree of Buddhahood (*tharmakaya*) cannot flower, cannot bare the fruit of the highest nirvana.

In the *Nirvana Sutra*[1] the Buddha clarifies the difference in perspective between the second and third round of teachings by stating that the first perspective, which denies the reality of that which is perceived by both the senses and the conceptual mind, was given as a medicine designed to cure the disciples of the suffering caused by grasping after the false appearances of self and phenomena. When it is clearly understood that they are not real, he tells us, desire for them naturally ceases. With the cessation of desire there arises a peace of the spirit in which emotions, desires and thoughts can no longer cloud the vision. "Only when the cure is complete," said the Buddha, "can the reality of the essential nature of beings be safely given. If the truth of the Buddha-principle is given too soon the disciples will cling to it."

Asanga, a direct disciple of Maitreya, in his commentary on this text, clarifies this further by quoting the Buddha's own words as recorded in the *Dharanisvara Sutra:*

> The Tathagata (Buddha), having perceived that the fundamental spiritual essence of beings is obscured through impurities, aroused in those who cling to material and conceptual existence an aversion to that existence by pointing out that it is impermanent, that it lacks a reality of its own, and that this false perception is the primary cause of their suffering. But the Tathagata did not stop there. He

---

[1] *Mahaparinirvanasutra*

then spoke of a spiritual awareness that is free of form, desire, and conceptual divisions. In this way he caused the disciples to perceive the Buddha-nature. But the Tathagata did not stop there. After this he expounded upon the supreme unity of subject, object, and activity, thereby causing the realization of the dharmakaya, the fully realized primordial awareness nature of a Buddha.

The Buddha taught that the essential nature of a Buddha and the essential nature of an ordinary human being are the same. The only difference is that a Buddha has removed the obscurations that hide it from view and an ordinary human being has not. The Buddha taught that this universal heart essence is, in a way inconceivable to the conceptual mind, our true identity (*svabhava*). In the final days before the Buddha passed into the unconditioned sphere of the highest nirvana he declared to those present that in order to clear up any remaining doubts he would answer any question put to him. He was then asked whether there is a self or not, a question that in the past he had often refused to answer directly.

> Oh good man, self (*atman*) means the tathagatagarbha, (the seed of buddhahood). This is the self. It has existed since the beginning but under cover of innumerable illusions.

That is why man cannot see it…. The 'self' spoken of in Buddhism is the Buddha-nature.[1]

The reason why the Buddha-nature is not usually described as a soul or self, even when realized as our true identity, is because it is not an isolated identity, as the term 'self' implies, but rather a universal principle. The 'Buddha' in Buddha-nature is not Gautama the person. It is the Buddha-principle within all beings. Eventually, as we follow the Mahayana path, the concept of the Buddha-nature, as an individual entity or self, disappears.

In the following treatise Maitreya identifies very briefly the ten bhumis or stages of enlightenment. The first stage involves identification with the pure Buddha-nature within oneself. The second level of enlightenment pertains to the realization of non-duality. The third level one attains spiritual freedom from the limitations of 'form, desire, and conceptual divisions.' The forth bhumi is reached through an identification with the Buddha-nature of all beings.

In the beginning of our search for this spiritual treasure a fundamental duality exists in the consciousness between the Buddha-principle itself and the seeker of it. Through meditation on the essential non-dual nature of awareness there eventually arises that unity of consciousness, which realizes that the awareness that perceives the spiritual nature and the spiritual nature itself is one and

---

[1] *Mahayana Mahaparinirvana Sutra.*

the same and that *this* is our true nature, our true identity, not as an isolated self but rather as a universal principle. "Awareness," says Maitreya, "lacks an observer."[1]

Beyond the illusion of appearances there is the clear perception of reality. Beyond the intellect there is primordial awareness. Beyond suffering there is the bliss of nirvana. Beyond impermanence there is the truth that does not change. And beyond the illusion of self lies the Heart Essence of all the Buddhas. The illusion of appearance takes place only in a deluded consciousness that does not yet perceive its true nature. It is therefore unworthy to classify the Buddhas and Bodhisattvas as phantoms, dreams, and illusions. The appearance of a Buddha or Bodhisattva is an illusion only to those who do not yet perceive their true nature. They are illusions, says Maitreya, only in the appearance of their form vehicles. As an example of this he states that the appearance in the world of the *sambhogakaya* vehicle of a Bodhisattva is an illusion because its true nature is hidden from view:

> Its manifestation is an illusion for like a gem that has been dyed various colors it does not visibly manifest its true nature. In the same way, though appearing in various forms according to the needs of sentient beings, the Lord (Buddha) never shows his true nature.[2]

---

[1] *The Middle Way*, 1-7

[2] 2- 52

The Blessed One has said:

> Ananda, the Buddha is invisible and cannot be seen
> with the eyes. Ananda, the Teachings of a Buddha
> cannot be uttered, nor can it be heard with the ears.
> Ananda, the Community of Bodhisattvas is spiritual by
> nature and cannot be approached with the body or
> (conceptual) mind.

In his chapter on the 'Qualities of a Buddha' Maitreya says:

> Just as in autumn on a cloudless day the image of the
> moon can be seen reflected in a pond, so the disciples
> of a Buddha perceived the manifestation of the
> omnipresent reflected in the body of a Buddha.

Latter in the same chapter Maitreya writes:

> The essential qualities of the dharmakaya are
> indivisible like space, while the two form bodies are
> like the appearance of the moon reflected in water.

In the *Shrimaladevi Sutra* the Buddha says that the fundamental
nature of a Buddha will not be understood by those who would
perceive it as an individual self, or by those "whose minds are
distracted with analytical conceptions of emptiness." The first is the

impurity of separateness. The second is the impurity of a conceptual, dualistic, rational mind view. The Buddha taught that the truth is beyond all words and concepts, even such exalted concepts as 'emptiness,' the 'Buddha-nature,' and the 'perfection of wisdom.'

> "Subhuti, the 'Perfection of Wisdom' is merely a name given to the teachings. It is not really the perfection of wisdom."[1]

The following verse from the *Mahaparinirvana Sutra* is said to be among the last words given by the Buddha before entering the highest nirvana. The Buddha-principle is here spoken of as the 'true nature of the mind.'

> Subhadra approached the Buddha.
> 'Oh World Honored One, how can we cut off all illusionary appearances?
> The Buddha answered, 'If a person meditates on the nature of the mind, such a person can cut off all illusionary appearances.'
> 'What is the nature of the mind?'
> 'The nature of the mind is its empty nature.'
> 'What is the empty nature of the mind?'

---

[1] The Diamond Cutter Sutra

'Good man, understand that nothing has any independent or isolated characteristics…. There is no division of any kind between seeing and the one who sees, between enlightenment and the one who is enlightened, between karma and the one who is responsible for the karma, between the defilements and the one who is defiled. The true nature of the mind is empty of all these conceptual divisions. All dualistic appearances are false. When these illusions are dissolved reality is perceived. This is the essential nature of the mind, the highest knowing, the dharmadhatu, the ultimate truth, and emptiness of the first magnitude.

The Sanskrit title for this teaching by Maitreya is *Ratnagotra-vibhaga*. '*Ratnagotra*' is an abbreviation for Buddharatnagotra, one of the names for the Buddha-nature. Literally it means the 'Buddha's Treasure Lineage.' 'Vibhaga' means a concise analysis or treatise. Asanga in his commentary on this teaching called it *Mahayana Uttaratantra*, or 'A Mahayana Teaching on the Supreme (*uttara*) Continuum (*tantra*).' Both of these titles refer to the Buddha-nature as a universal continuum.

Maitreya, for the sake of clarity, divides the indivisible Treasure Lineage into seven essential spheres of Buddhahood (*vajrapadas*): (1) The Buddha, (2) The Buddha's Teaching, (3) The Community of Bodhisattvas, (4) The Seed of Buddhahood, (5) Enlightenment, (6)

The Quality of a Buddha (7) The Activity of a Buddha. These seven vajrapadas form the seven chapters of the work.

Maitreya defines the term 'vajra' in this teaching by comparing it to the superhuman faculties of a fully enlightened Buddha: "They are like a vajra in that they are indestructible, essential, eternal, and unchanging." As Jamgon Kongtrul points out in his commentary on this text, the term 'vajra,' when used in Buddhism, generally represents the *Buddhavajra*, the 'indestructible Buddha-essence.' In this text the seven vajrapadas all represent the essential nature of buddhahood from different perspectives or phases of its realization, beginning with the cause and ending in the fruit. The fourth vajrapada, for example, is *dhatu*, which is an abbreviation for Buddhadhatu, the essential element of buddhahood latent, unrealized, and hidden within all beings. It is the pure impulse behind the spiritual evolution of consciousness. It is hidden because the impurities that cover it hide it from view. A Buddha, the first and highest vajrapada, is the dharmakaya, the complete realization of the Buddha-nature, where all the impurities that previously hid it from view have been removed, thus making possible other perspectives of the Buddhavajra, which include the 'teachings,' the 'awakened disciples,' 'enlightenment,' the 'quality of a Buddha,' and the 'activity of a Buddha.' In this way all seven essential spheres of Buddhahood are in fact the Buddha Nature at some level or stage of its uncovering and manifestation.

My prayer is that the good energies that will certainly arise from the study and application of this precious teaching go toward the liberation of all beings from ignorance and suffering.

OM Svabhava Shuddha Sarva Dharma Svabhavo Shuddha HUM
Naturally pure is all phenomena. Naturally pure am I.[1]

---

[1] This mantra, along with its translation, was given by H. H. the 14th Dalai Lama at the end of a lengthy series of teachings given in Los Angeles, California.

The Buddha Nature

Ratnagotravibhaga
A Concise Teaching on the Treasure Lineage

Chapter 1

The Seven Essential Spheres of Buddhahood

This work briefly illuminates the seven fundamental spheres of Buddhahood.

1) A Buddha

2) The Teachings of a Buddha (*dharma*)

3) The Community of Bodhisattvas (*sangha*)

4) The Seed of a Buddhahood within all beings (*dhatu*)

5) Enlightenment (*bodhi*)

6) The Qualities of a Buddha (*guna*)

7) The Activity of a Buddha (*karma*)

The first three were taught by the Buddha in his introduction to the *Dharanisvara Raja Pariprccha*, the final four were taught in a later chapter of the same work on understanding the difference between a Buddha and a Bodhisattva.

They have a natural progression: From the Buddha arises his teaching. From the teaching arises the spiritual community of enlightened Bodhisattvas. Present within the community of Bodhisattvas there exists the Buddha-nature. The Buddha-nature manifests as the enlightenment, the qualities and the spiritual activities of a Buddha.

The Buddha, the First Vajrapada

I bow to the Buddha,

Who is without beginning, center, or end,

Whose mind is at peace,

Who has fully realized the Buddha-nature,

Who, having attained enlightenment, fearlessly reveals to the ignorant ones the path to spiritual freedom,

Who, with the sword of compassionate activity, and the clearly perceived diamond of truth, cuts down the forest of (illusory) phenomena,

Who destroys the walls of doubt and the thickets of conceptual divisions.

His essential nature is not subject to change.

His actions are spontaneous and without premeditation.

His view is not dependent upon an outside source.

He is endowed with wisdom, compassion, and power.

He pursues the twofold aim (the liberation of self and others).

The Buddha is not subject to change because (essentially) he has no beginning, center, or end.   1/5

His mind is quiescent and his actions are spontaneous and without forethought because he has attained the dharmakaya, the full flowering perfection of the seed of buddhahood.

His essential nature is realized, not through an outside source, but from within.

He demonstrates wisdom by manifesting the three primary qualities; power, wisdom, and compassionate activity.

He demonstrates compassionate activity by showing the way.

He demonstrates power by destroying the obstructing force, the illusionary appearance of phenomena.

The first three (the unchanging nature, quiescence, and enlightenment) are developed for one's own benefit.

The latter three (power, wisdom, and compassionate activity) are developed to benefit others.

The Second Vajrapada
The Teachings of a Buddha

I bow to the truth of the (Buddha)-dharma, which like the sun illuminates the consciousness:

It is neither non-relative nor relative.

It is not non-relative and relative together.

It is not other than non-relative and relative.[1]

It cannot be analyzed nor defined in words.

It can only be realized directly by a mind that is quiescent and pure.

It is realized through primordial wisdom.

The teachings of a Buddha, like rays of light, destroy the desires, hatred, and ignorance that fill samsara, the ocean of conditioned existence.

The teachings of a Buddha illuminate the two truths:

1. The (non-relative) truth that does not change, that is the cessation of suffering, that is beyond all concepts and dualities, and that is pure and clear

2. The (relative) truth of the path   1/10

Liberation from the limitations of ignorance is attained by understanding both of these truths.[2]

The two truths each have three qualities.

The sun-like qualities (of the truth of the path) are:

1. Purity

---

[1] A similar teaching can be found in the *Lankavatara Sutra* where they are called the 'four negations' (*catuskotika*). They point to the essential nature of reality (*tathata*) as 1. Not unity or diversity, 2) Not manifested (matter) or unmanifested (spirit), 3) Not eternal or non-eternal, and 4) not both (of these together) or other (than these).

[2] "Conceptual wisdom," says Maitreya "leads to spiritual freedom. Non-conceptual wisdom is spiritual freedom."

2. Clarity

3. A quiescent mind

This leads to the (non-relative) truth, which is:

1. Beyond words

2. Beyond duality

3. Beyond all conceptual divisions

The Third Vajrapada
The Community of Enlightened Bodhisattvas

I bow to the Sangha, the Community of enlightened Bodhisattvas.

Who by directing their pure awareness within have irreversibly attained the supreme qualities.

Who have realized that though the exterior world is an illusion, its essential nature is quiescent and pure.

Who realize that all impurities lack reality.

And who, through the purity of clear light awareness, understand perfectly that the essential nature of all beings is infinite and pure and that this essence of Buddhahood is universally present in all the people of the world.

Who have realized the quiescent innate purity of the essential nature of phenomena.   1/15

Who have perfectly realized the essential awareness nature of all beings through wisdom that is all-inclusive.

This realization, which arises from the awareness of the immaculate expanse of their wisdom, is free from all attachments and obstructions.

Since the wisdom of the Bodhisattvas, like that of a Buddha, is pure, their attainment is irreversible.

Therefore, they are a refuge for all living beings.

The Three Jewels

Those who strive to attain the virtuous activity of the three vehicles of a Buddha find refuge in the Buddha, the Dharma, and the Sangha.

The Dharma and the Sangha (however) do not represent the supreme refuge. This is because the Dharma, the teachings, (like all conceptual phenomena) is not (ultimately) real and will therefore perish, and the Sangha, the spiritual community, is not free (of samsara). 1/20 The absolute refuge for all living beings is the dharmakaya Buddha, the highest goal of the disciples.

(The Buddha, the Dharma, and the Sangha) are like jewels because they are beautiful, pure, rare, powerful, (essentially) unchanging and of the highest perfection. These three rare and most beautiful Jewels, as well as the qualities of a Buddha, his activity, and enlightenment, arise from the ultimate nature reality itself (*tathata*), which is (at first) hidden by impurities but is then uncovered and clearly perceived.

The essential nature of the three Jewels is perceived through the all-seeing awareness nature (of a Buddha).

The Last Four Vajrapadas

The (last) four (vajrapadas, the Buddha-nature, bodhi-enlightenment, the qualities of a Buddha, and the activity of a Buddha) are difficult to understand for four reasons.

1. That which is to be realized (the Buddha-nature), while pure is (nevertheless) covered (hidden) by impurities.

2. Realization (Enlightenment) is the absence of these impurities.

3. The qualities of a Buddha, brought about through realization, cannot (as it seems) be divided into individual characteristics.

4. The manifested result of realization (the activity of a Buddha) is spontaneous and unpremeditated.   1/25

The first (the seed of buddhahood) is to be purified.

The last three (enlightenment, qualities, and activity) arise when the impurities (that hide the Buddha-nature) have been removed.

The Forth Vajrapada
The Seed of Buddhahood

Because the perfectly pure, all-inclusive, wisdom nature of a Buddha is universally present in all beings, and since its pure being nature cannot be divided into parts, and since it is the root source of buddhahood, it is named the Buddha-nature after its fruit (a Buddha). Everyone can realize it because, as the Buddha has said, all beings have the Buddha-dahtu within them.

Its nature can be approached from the following perspectives:

As one's true nature or identity (*svabhava*)

As the root cause

As the final result

Through its manifested activity

As indivisible unity

As various levels of awareness

As all-pervasive

As unchanging,

As being indivisible

As the highest absolute element of a Buddha (*para-martha-dhatu*)

The Buddha-nature can be likened to a jewel, to space, and to pure water. It is like a wish-fulfilling jewel for its nature is made powerful with reverent faith in the teachings. Its nature is perceived by an exalted consciousness in meditation to be like space, unchanging, infinite, and all-inclusive. It is like pure water for it is free of poison and moist with compassion.   1/30

The Four Obstructions to the Realization of the Buddha Nature

The four obstructions to the realization of the Buddha-nature include:

    1. An aversion to the teachings

    2. A self-centered perspective

    3. The fear of pain

    4. An indifference to the welfare of others

The first of these (an aversion to the teachings) applies mainly to worldly people who have little understanding. The second (a self-centered perspective) applies to heretics who perceive an independent ego. The third (the fear of pain) applies to the Sravakas, who (perceiving the world to be filled with suffering) fear suffering. And the forth obstruction (a lack of compassion) applies to the Pratyekabuddhas, (who seek liberation for their self alone).

The Dharmakaya is the Result of Purification

There are four ways that one can be purified of these obstructions:

1. (An aversion to the teachings is overcome) through reverent faith.

2. (A self-centered perspective is overcome) by developing pure virtue.

3. (A fear of pain is overcome) through meditation.

4. (An indifference to the welfare of others is destroyed) through compassionate activity.

The cause of a bodhisattva is reverent faith in the Mahayana teachings.

The mother, who gives birth to the quality of a Buddha, is wisdom.

The womb (from which this birth takes place) is the bliss of meditation.

The nurse (who gives nourishment to the bodhisattvas) is compassionate activity.

The result of (psychic) purification is the attainment of the perfect qualities of a Buddha: Purity (of consciousness), an understanding of one's essential nature, bliss, immortality, non-attraction to samsara, and a striving for and a heartfelt attraction to the peace (of nirvana).   1/35

Through the diligent application of the four qualities given above, as antidotes to the four obstructions, the dharmakaya is attained. Devotion to the teachings overcomes an aversion to the teachings. Wisdom overcomes a self-centered perspective. Meditation overcomes a fear of pain. Compassionate activity overcomes an indifference to the suffering of others.

The Dharmakaya is the Buddha Nature uncovered

The dharmakaya is doubly pure. 1) It is inherently pure. 2) And it is pure because the samskaras, (the psychic impurities, habitual tendencies and the conditioned imprints) that covered it, have all been removed.

The dharmakaya is the highest synthesis. It transcends the duality of self and others. Because of this it remains eternally quiescent. It is supreme bliss because all conceptual divisions have been removed, along with the root cause of those divisions. It is eternal because it transcends the duality of samsara and nirvana.

The Great Bodhisattvas remain in Samsara for the sake of Sentient Beings.

The great Bodhisattvas, in their wisdom, have rejected all forms of self-love. Because of this and because of the great love they have for all beings they do not enter the supreme peace (of the highest nirvana). By combining a love for others with wisdom, they aid others to attain supreme enlightenment. And though they abide in samsara they are not conditioned by it.

Does the Buddha Nature Exist?

If the Buddha-nature did not exist there would be no impulse to be liberated from the suffering of samsara and no heartfelt attraction to nirvana. 1/40 Manifested existence (samsara) is full of suffering and is therefore impure, Nirvana is bliss and therefore has merit; neither would exist without the Buddhadhatu inherent (within all beings).

Like a great ocean the Buddha-essence contains immeasurable precious and inexhaustible treasures. Like a lantern it illuminates these treasure as being indivisible with itself.

The dharmakaya is the essential nature and root source of a Buddha's compassion. For this reason it has been likened to a treasure in the ocean, as well as the watery container of the treasure (the ocean itself).

The dharmakaya is the essential nature and root source of wisdom and pure clairvoyant vision. For this reason it has been likened to a lamp as well as the light, heat, and color (of the lamp).

The Buddha Nature,
Though Essentially the Same in all Beings Manifests Differently.

The essential nature of a Buddha, the essential nature of a Bodhisattva, and the essential nature of an ordinary person is the same indivisible Buddha-nature. Yet it is only the perfect Buddhas that perceive it clearly.   1/45

In ordinary beings its manifestation is distorted.

In exalted beings it manifests clearly without any distortion.

In a Buddha it manifests in complete freedom from all psychic impurities, concepts, and conditioning.

In ordinary beings it is veiled by impurities.

In exalted beings it is unveiled and pure.

The Buddha Nature cannot be divided into parts.

In a Buddha it is absolutely pure.

In the same way that space, which is all-pervasive, cannot be divided into parts, so the Buddha-nature, which is the all-pervasive essential nature of the mind, cannot be divided into parts.

The Buddha Nature is Not Polluted by Ignorance.

In the same way that space encompasses all things—the inferior, the average, and the supreme—and is not polluted by them because of its subtle nature, so the Buddha-nature (though it encompasses both faults and virtues) remains absolutely pure.

In the same way that worlds arise and disappear in space yet space remains unchanged by it, so the perception of the senses arise in the mind yet its unconditioned essential nature remains unchanged by it.

In the same way that fire cannot affect space, so the fire of sickness, old age and death cannot affect the Buddha-essence.

Above the earth is water. Above the water is air. Above the air is space. And above space there is not anything. 1/55 The material world is like the earth. The world of psychic conditioning and desire is like the water. The sphere of conceptual thinking is like air. The pure sphere, the essential nature of the mind, is like space.

Material forms are dependent upon the forces of karmic conditioning and psychic (emotional) impurities. Karmic conditioning and the emotional impurities (desire) are dependent upon the activity of thought. The activity of thought is a (distorted) reflection of the primordial mind, which is pure. The primordial mind, like space, is not dependent upon anything.

From the primordial mind arises the conceptual mind. From the conceptual mind arises the basis for the forces of karma, psychic impurities, and desire. 1/60 From the water-like forces of karma and emotional impurities arises the appearance and disappearance of material forms.

The Buddha Nature as the Primordial Mind

The primordial mind is unconditioned, like space, having no cause, no characteristics, and no parts. It has no beginning or end. The primordial Buddha-essence, like space, has no opposite. It is luminous. It cannot be changed into anything else. And though completely pure in itself, it is nevertheless covered with the impurities of karma, ego-desire and conceptual thinking. And though it is covered by these water-like impurities, it is not effected by them.[1] It is also unaffected by the three fires of samsara—illness, old age and death. These three fires correspond to ordinary fire, the fire of hell, and the fire of pralaya (the final dissolution of the phenomenal worlds). 1/65

---

[1] Longchenpa gives an analogy to explain this seeming paradox. When we see the reflection of our face in the mirror our face does not really enter the mirror at all. In the same way when we see the reflection of the dharmadhatu as phenomena in the mind, the dharmadhatu does not actually enter the mirror of the conceptual mind at all. It is therefore not polluted by it. To think we actually see our face in the mirror is an illusion. To think that we actually see reality in phenomena is likewise an illusion.

The Bodhisattvas Remain in Samsara to help Liberate Beings.

The Bodhisattvas, having realized the pure reality of their essential nature, are liberated from (the necessity of) birth, illness, old age, and death. But due to their great compassion they nevertheless remain (for a time) in the world of birth, illness, old age and death (for the sake of sentient beings). Although these heirs of the Victorious One have directly realized the essential nature of the world, they nevertheless appear to be subjected to birth (illness, old-age, and death). It is amazing that having attained the level of an enlightened Bodhisattva they nevertheless appear as ordinary beings! They are called *Friends of the World* because they have united wisdom with the highest level of compassionate activity. 1/70 Though they are superior to all other people they are not separate from them.

The Bodhisattvas, though they continuously work to benefit the world, remain unaffected by it. Just as a lotus flower grows in (muddy) water and yet is not polluted by it, so the great Bodhisattvas live in the world and yet are not polluted by it. In quiet meditation they utilize the pure psychic energy of the mind for the benefit (of the world). Through the power of this accumulated energy they lead all sentient beings to maturity, spontaneously and without forethought.

The Bodhisattvas know intuitively who are to be taught and by what means and manner. 1/75 They therefore teach, act, practice, and appear in their two form-vehicles (physical and etheric) accordingly. This is done spontaneously with unobstructed wisdom for the benefit of all beings in the universe as vast as space.

The difference between Buddhas and Bodhisattvas

The Bodhisattvas are equal to the Buddha in their ability to convey beings to the other shore. Yet the difference between a Buddha and a Bodhisattva is as great as the difference between an atom and the world itself, or between the water that has accumulated in the footprint of a bull and the ocean.

The Buddha Nature

The essential nature of a Buddha is unchanging and eternal.

It is a refuge to the world for it is unlimited by time.

It is without duality for it is beyond all conceptual divisions. 1/80

Not having been created, it cannot be destroyed. It will not end even in the great indefinable transformation (of nirvana).

Being quiescent it experiences no suffering from illness arising from the (karmic) forces of psychic impurities.

It does not experience death or aging for it is not subject to the force of karma.

Thus we see that the unconditioned is eternal, etc. (beyond conceptual division, free of birth, suffering, old age, and death).

The Unity of the Dharmakaya, Buddha, Non-relative Truth, and Nirvana

The dharmakaya, the essential nature of a Buddha, non-relative truth, and nirvana are as inseparable as the rays of the sun. And though they each express different aspects of the dharmadhatu, the pure Sphere of Reality, these four are nevertheless synonymous.[1] Without a Buddha there is no nirvana. 1/85 From the highest perspective the Buddha and nirvana are one and the same unsurpassable enlightened awareness (*dharmakaya*), which is the absence of the 'root of impurities' (ignorance).

All of the Six Perfections are Necessary

A king once asked a group of painters to paint his portrait. But because each one could paint only a certain part of the body, and because one of the painters had left the country, the portrait could not be completed.

The painters represent the six perfections:

    1. Generosity,

    2. Ethics,

---

[1] The divine perceiver, enlightened perception, the object of enlightened perception and it's fruit are, in the last analysis, one and the same.

3. Patience, and the rest.

(4. Effort,

5. Meditation,

6. Transcendental wisdom.) 1/90

With the absence of but one of the six perfections, the portrait, representing the realization of unconditioned being, cannot be completed.

The mind of wisdom and (the act of) liberation are as inseparable as rays of the sun, brilliant, radiant, and clear.[1]

Just as one cannot see the sun without first perceiving its rays, so one cannot enter nirvana without first becoming a Buddha.

Parables concerning the Hidden Buddha Nature

The Buddha-essence has been explained above in ten ways. It is hidden from view by psychic impurities. This has been illuminated (by the Buddha) through the following parables.[2] 1/95

Suppose a Buddha, radiant with purified qualities, was to abide in a lotus flower. And suppose a seer with pure vision could see him there and could separate him from the wilted petals. In the same way the Buddha, with the eyes of wisdom, perceives the spiritual essence within the beings of the lower worlds. And because he is pure,

---

[1] Wisdom and skillful means.

[2] These parables are quoted by Maitreya directly from the Buddha's sutra teachings of the third round.

immortal, and compassionate he liberates them from the obscurations.

Suppose a clever person, having seen some honey surrounded by a swarm of bees, obtained the honey by skillfully separating them. In the same way a great Sage with omniscient vision perceiving the honey-like pure spiritual essence, attains it by completely removing the beelike impurities (that cover it).

Nourishing grain is covered by a hard shell. To eat it, therefore, one must first remove it from the husk. In the same way the kernel of buddhahood within all beings must be removed from the polluted stains (that cover it) before it can be utilized in the compassionate activity of a Buddha in the three worlds (of samsara). The kernels of grain cannot be made sweet without first removing the husks.

In the same way the Lord of Dharma, residing in all beings, gives (spiritual) nourishment to those who hunger by liberating them from the husk of impurities. 1/107

Suppose a traveler happened to drop a piece of gold in a pile of garbage where it remained hidden for hundreds of years without any change. And suppose a god with pure vision saw it and said to the people; "Look, here is pure gold the most precious of substances, remove it from the garbage and make use of it." In the same way the Buddha, perceiving that the gold-like quality in all living beings is immersed in garbage-like (psychic) impurities, pours the Mahayana Teachings over the living beings to wash them clean of their impurities. Just as the god perceiving the beautiful gold that had fallen in the garbage told the people to clean and use it, so the Buddha, perceiving that the treasure of the Buddha-nature in living beings was immersed in impurities, taught the Dharma in order to purify the treasure. 1/111

Now suppose there was a large treasure of jewels hidden in the ground beneath the house of a poor man. But the man did not know of this treasure. In the same way hidden in the ground of all beings there is the indefinable and inexhaustible treasure of (primordial) mind. The people of the world, who do not know of this treasure, experience the suffering of spiritual poverty in various ways. To enable the people, who are likened to the poor man in the parable, to obtain the treasure of mind the Sage made his appearance in the world.

The seed of the fruit of a Mango tree is of an imperishable nature. When planted in the soil and watered and when it has received the light of the sun, it will grow into the king of trees. In the same way, the pure imperishable nature abiding in all living beings and covered by the skin of ignorance, when watered by virtue and exposed to the light of the dharma, will grow into the king of sages.

Reverence and Faith

The essential nature of a Buddha can only be realized through reverence and faith in its reality, for without the eyes of reverence and faith one cannot perceive the radiant sphere of this sun-like Buddha-essence.

It must be perceived as it truly is, without anything added or taken away. One who perceives truth in this way attains liberation.

The Buddha's Teachings of the Second and Third Round

In the Buddha's earlier teachings (of the second round) he said that all appearances are unreal, being like clouds, like visions in a dream and like an illusion. So how is it that the Lord declares here (in the third cycle of teachings) that the Buddha-nature exists in all beings? The Buddha-nature is empty of all (conceptual) divisions and impurities. It is not empty of the highest. It is indivisible with it.   1-155

In the (Buddha's) earlier teaching (of the second round) he taught that the appearance of phenomena, produced by the samskaras are like clouds and so forth, devoid of reality; and that these impurities are (also) like clouds, dreams and illusions; and that the (five) elements magically appear like illusions.

Problems Arising from the Buddha's Second Round of Teachings

Through these earlier teachings (of the second round) five negative reactions have arisen.

    1. Feelings of futility.

2. Contempt for inferior people.

3. A fixation on illusions.

4. A disparaging attitude toward the reality of one's essential nature.

5. Cherishing self more than others.

To remove these five defects the Buddha taught the truth of the Buddha-nature, which is his ultimate doctrine.   1-160

Some people upon hearing the earlier teaching (on emptiness), and not having heard the latter teachings (on the Buddha-nature), are overcome with feelings of futility.[1] Because of this they do not develop the bodhichitta, the pure impulse to attain enlightenment for the sake of others. And if this impulse does arise within them they are apt to become proud of it, saying 'I am superior to those whose minds have not attained the pure motivating impulse to attain enlightenment.'[2]

True insight does not arise in those who think in this way, and they therefore continue to cling to the illusions and do not perceive their true nature.

The impurities of living beings are unnatural and unreal, yet the essential nature of these impurities, though empty of material and conceptual reality, are nevertheless real. From the Buddha-nature arise the qualities of a Buddha, the essential nature of which is also

___

[1] Subhuti asked the Buddha, "If sentient beings do not really exist, why should we strive for enlightenment in order to liberate them?"

[2] The later teachings remove this feeling of superiority by teaching that the Buddha Nature is *equally* present in all beings.

pure. If an intelligent person, while understanding that the impurities are not real, believes also that the essential nature of a Buddha and innate qualities of a Buddha are unreal, he cannot attain that benevolence which regards all living beings as equal to himself.[1]

Upon hearing these teachings (on the Buddha-nature) there arises great joy, respect for the Buddha, conceptual wisdom, primordial wisdom, and love (for all beings).

The five defects are thereby replaced by:

1) (Feeling of futility are replaced by) a powerful motivation to follow the spiritual path for the sake of others (*bodhichitta*).

2. (Contempt for inferior people is replaced by) a love for all beings.

3. (Fixation on the illusion of phenomena is replaced by) prajna, the realization of the fundamental nature of phenomena.

4. (The disparaging of the Buddha-nature is replaced by) wisdom (*jnana*).

5. (Cherishing self more than others is replaced by) compassion.

Through these five qualities one is liberated from these five defects and attains equanimity. Thus one realizes the absence of impurities and the presence of the pure qualities of a Buddha. With love one understands the true equality of self and others. In this way

---

[1] Jamgon Kongtrul says that it is through the teachings on the Buddha-nature that we come to realize that the true nature of self and the true nature others are the same.

one becomes free of the five defects and attains a realization of the essential nature of Buddhahood at an early date.

Chapter 2

The Buddha Nature Uncovered

The Ten Bhumis or Stages of Enlightenment[1]

1. (Realization of) Innate purity (of the Buddha-nature)

2. Opposites exist only in the mind[2]

3. Spiritual freedom[3]

4. Identification with (the Buddha-nature in) all beings

5. The essential nature of consciousness (*asraya*)[4]

6. Innate altruism (selflessness).

7. The vast expanse.

8. Infinity.

9. Omnipresence

10. The essential nature of reality itself (*tathata*)[5]

---

[1] These are given in the order of attainment from the lowest to the highest.

[2] Asanga interprets this verse as relating to the perfect integration of conceptual wisdom and non-conceptual wisdom.

[3] Liberation from the conditioning effects of ignorance and psychic impurities.

[4] Asanga says that '*asraya*' is a synonym for *alayavijnana*, the root or basis of consciousness.

[5] I have translated the term 'tathata' as the 'essential nature of reality' rather than 'as it is,' or the ambiguous 'suchness,' which is usual. A more literal, and perhaps more accurate, translation might be 'pure being' or Be-ness. 'Tatha' means 'being.' The suffix 'ta' here means 'ness' or 'nature of.'

1. (The primordial purity of the Buddha-nature) is one's own essential nature (*svabhava*).

2. (The realization of non-duality) is the cause.

3. (Spiritual freedom) is the result.

4. (Identification with Buddha-nature in all beings) produces altruistic activity,

5. (The essential nature of the mind) is supreme unity

6-8. (Infinity, the vast expanse, and innate altruism) manifests (for the benefit of others) as the three vehicles of a Buddha).

9. (Spontaneous omnipresence) is eternal.

10. (The essential nature of reality) is indefinable.

These (10) points demonstrate the stages of the Buddha's enlightenment.

The first stage, the realization of doubly pure Buddha Nature

The innate purity of the Buddha-nature is radiant like the sun and all pervasive like space. And though obscured by a multitude of cloud-like impurities and unnatural perceptions, it is nevertheless eternally present and without change. When fully realized through both non-conceptual wisdom and purified conceptual wisdom, it manifests as the pure qualities of a Buddha.

The Buddha Essence is doubly pure because it is indivisible (innately pure) and because it has the (acquired purity) of the virtuous qualities of a Buddha. The first purity is non-conceptual wisdom. It is like space. (infinite, all encompassing, and indivisible). The second purity, which is the result of the removal (of the psychic impurities), is like the sun, (radiant) with the manifesting qualities of a Buddha as numerous as the sands of the Ganga.   2/5

The (two) veils (preventing clear insight) are

   1) Psychic impurities

   2) Ignorance.

They are like the clouds (that hide the sun). The dissolving of these two kinds of veils is attained through both non-conceptual and conceptual wisdom.

Meaning of the Parables

The meaning of the parables (given above), that the Buddha-nature is like a treasure, (etc.)…(is as follows):

The Buddha-nature is absolutely pure.

It is spiritual freedom.

It is the essential nature of all beings.

It is indestructible, eternal, quiescent, constant, and unchanging.

It is the source and cause of sentiency.

It is the source of the miraculous display of forms perceived by the six sense organs.[1]

It is the pure scent of the Buddha's morality.

---

[1] The 6th sense organ, the rational mind, is the sense that coordinates the other five.

It is the pure taste of the sublime doctrine of the noble ones.

It is the touch of bliss during samadhi.

It is the realization of the supreme bliss nature of the Tathagata himself, which, like space does not change.   2/20

The Result of the Two-fold Wisdom

In brief, the application of the two-fold wisdom (purified conceptual and innately pure non-conceptual wisdom) leads to the manifestation of two vehicles (respectively):

(1) The vimuktikaya, which is the (vehicle for the) totally spontaneous activity of spiritual freedom

(2) The dharmakaya, the primordially pure fully realized wisdom nature of Buddha

And though they are presented here in terms of two vehicles (wisdom and activity) they are essentially the same, uncreated, unpolluted, all-pervading fundamental nature. The vimuktikaya vehicle is free because it has been purified of all psychic impurities. It is therefore not hindered, obstructed, or conditioned by them.[1] The dharmakaya is the all-pervasive primordial wisdom of a Buddha.

The destruction of the impurities results in four freedoms:

1) Freedom from decay

2) Freedom from change

---

[1] Jamgon Kongtrul comments: "By meditating with equipoise upon Pure Being Reality (*tathata*) one attains perfect non-attachment. This is a manifestation of the Vimuktikaya, the vehicle of complete liberation from all objects of attachment."

3) Freedom from divisions

4) Freedom from the necessity of rebirth

Since it is free of these things it is known to be:

1. Everlastingly pure

2) Unchanging

3) Indivisible

4) At peace

The dharmakaya is called *the basis* because it supports and is the source of all the qualities of a Buddha.

In the same way that space has no cause and yet allows for the seeing of forms, the hearing of sounds, of taste, smells, and substances to touch, so this twofold manifestation of a Buddha allows for the natural unstained Buddha qualities to arise.

The (doubly) pure essential nature of a Buddha is indefinable, eternal, permanent, quiescent, continual, and unchanging. Like space it is all-pervasive, without conceptual divisions, attachments, or hindrances. Like space it cannot be seen or grasped. Like space it is free from all impurities.

The two manifestations of the essential nature of a Buddha (*dharmakaya* and *vimuktikaya*) bring benefit to one's self and others. In this way it brings benefit to all. 2/30

The Essential Nature of a Buddha is Inconceivable.

The essential nature of a Buddha is realized only through primordial wisdom and is not the object of the three kinds of acquired knowledge. It is so subtle that even those with a very high intellect cannot perceive it. As it is supreme[1] truth it cannot be analyzed, nor can it be attained by merely thinking about it. It is like something invisible to one born blind, or like the sun to a newborn baby that has not yet left the house.

The essential nature of a Buddha is eternal because it has not been created.

It is permanent because it cannot be destroyed.

It is quiescent because it is free (of the friction) of duality.

It is continual because the nature of reality always remains unchanged.

It is at peace because it is the noble truth of the cessation of suffering.

It is all-pervasive because of its nature is like space.

It is without any conceptual divisions, attachments, or hindrances because all the samskaras[2] have been removed.

---

[1] Non-conceptual.

[2] Samskaras are psychic conditioning (emotional as well as conceptual) that we cling to due our attachments to them. Psychologists appropriately call them 'baggage'.

It cannot be seen because it is immaterial.

It cannot be grasped (conceptually) because it does not have any parts or divisions.

It is pure because that is its nature.

It is (also) pure because all the impurities that hid it from view have been removed.

The Dharmadhatu and the Buddha Nature are essentually the same.

The dharmadhatu, the essential nature of phenomena, is without beginning, middle, or end. It is indivisible, non-dual, and pure. It is not perceived by the conceptual mind though a yogi can realize it through one-pointed meditation. It is the same as the pure essential nature of all the Buddhas, naturally arising when the samskaras are removed and the inconceivable, unequalled, qualities of a Buddha, as innumerable as the sands of the Ganga, are realized.

The Nature of the Form Bodies of a Buddha

A Buddha works for the liberation of the world. He is like a king with a wish-fulfilling gem, magically appearing in his rainbow body and other forms. But these form vehicles do not constitute his true nature. 2/40 He appears in his archetypal form body[1] (*bimba*) to guide the disciples on the path that leads to peace, to develop them fully, to give prophecy, and to be the cause of their liberation. The form bodies of the Buddhas (through which they gives aid) remain with the world, as they are a part of.[2]

The Svabhavikakaya[3]

The Svabha-vika-kaya is the vehicle through which the awareness of infinity, the highest inconceivable realization of absolute truth, and the complete absence of all suffering, arises. It is realized as being one's own essential nature (*svabha*). And while it is indivisible, it can (for the sake of clarity) be divided into three Buddha vehicles (*kayas*), which arise from (the realization of) the infinity, vast expanse, and innate altruism, (as given above).

(The realization of infinity gives rise to the dharmakaya. The realization of the universal vast expanse gives rise to the sambhogakaya. The realization of one's innate altruistic nature gives rise to the nirmanakaya.)

The svabhavika-kaya has five characteristics:

1. It is totally indivisible, unchanging, and nondual.

---

[1] The bimba(-kaya) also known as the 'vajra body' and 'the pure illusion body,' is the archetype of the physical body, which is called the 'impure illusion body.' It is considered by some to be identical with the nirmanakaya. It might also be called the 'etheric body.'

[2] The subtle bodies of the Buddha do not follow him into the Higher Sphere of Parinirvana.

[3] The 'svabhavika-kaya,' is considered by some to be a synonym for the dharmakaya.

2. It is liberated from the three veils of psychic impurities, ignorance and the obstructions (distractions) to meditative equipoise.

3. It is liberated from the delusion of conceptual divisions.

4. It is the yogi's true field of the experience.

5. It is pure luminous clarity. 2/45

These characteristics, which are the greatest qualities of a Buddha, are immeasurable, inconceivable, incomparable, and totally pure.

Sambhogakaya

Due to the compassionate nature of the sambhogakaya, the vehicle of heart felt joy, it naturally, spontaneously, and continuously manifests itself for the benefit of those beings that seek (liberation). Because its power is like that of a wish-fulfilling gem, it appears (to the disciples in various ways) in a vision, in visible form, in the act of teaching, etc. Its manifestation is an illusion because like a gem that has been dyed various colors it does not manifest its essential nature. In the same way, though appearing in various forms according to the need of sentient beings, the Lord (Buddha) never shows his true nature.

Nirmanakaya

Knowing the nature of the world, and having compassion for (the beings of) the world, (a Buddha) manifests in (the world through) various nirmanakaya forms. This he does without ever leaving the undivided, unconditioned dharmakaya.

From the Tushita-heavens he descended to his mother's womb and was born. He then gained skill in various crafts, sciences, and the arts. He enjoyed his spouse and her entourage. Wearying of this he renounced desire and followed the path of asceticism. At the *Seat of the Awakened Heart*[1] he mastered the dark forces of Mara and attained perfect enlightenment. 2-55 After giving several rounds of teachings, he then passed into parinirvana, the highest enlightenment.

As long as there are living beings in the three worlds that are infested with impurities, a Buddha will manifest in this way, using words (such as) impermanent, suffering, selflessness, and quiescence. He will know how to direct them to nirvana.

False Enlightenment

For those who have attained quiescence and (mistakenly) think that they have attained nirvana, the Buddha gave teachings (such as) the *White Lotus Sutra* and others, wherein conceptual wisdom and

---

[1] The place of the Buddha's enlightenment.

skillful means was taught, to mature the disciple and to prepare him or her for the realization of the highest vehicle. He then gave prophecy concerning their eventual enlightenment.

The Three Vehicles of a Buddha

Since (the three vehicles of the Buddhas) are profoundly subtle, powerful and labor endlessly to benefit beings, they are known as universal, infinite, and deeply profound. 2/60 The first is the dharmakaya, the primordial wisdom vehicle of a Buddha. The latter (two) are the form vehicles; and though these two are (sometimes) visible[1] and abide in space, they are (nevertheless) inseparable from the first (the formless dharmakaya).

Why Buddhas Manifest in the World

The Lords endlessly appear in the world because the number of living beings is great. With compassion, miraculous power, indivisible wisdom and bliss, and by mastering the (Mahayana) teachings and defeating demon death, they offer their bodies, their lives, and their goods, to benefit all living beings. By preserving the sacred doctrine and to fulfill their original vows they manifest the compassion of (the two purities), the innate purity (of the Buddha-nature) and the developed purity (when it is unveiled). Through this (two fold) wisdom they are freed from the duality of samsara and nirvana. 2/65

---

[1] The sambhogakaya is said to be visible to one who has attained clairvoyant vision.

They manifest the highest bliss of Samadhi, which is beyond all conceptual divisions. And because their (minds) are quiescent and because they have conquered death they are not affected by the worldly phenomena. Because of this the Buddhas endlessly give refuge to those who need shelter.

The first seven points clarify the reasons for endlessly manifesting in their form bodies. The latter three illustrate the ever-present nature of the dharmakaya.

The Essential Nature of Reality is Inconceivable

The essential nature of reality *(tathata)* is inconceivable (not perceived as a concept). It is not encompassed by either samsara or nirvana. Even the great Rishis, the highest Bodhisattvas, do not understand it (completely). It is inconceivable because it cannot be understood by the conceptual mind. 2/70

It is the supreme, the highest truth and cannot be expressed in words. It is not encompassed by the merits of the one (nirvana) or the defects of the other (samsara). The first of these points concern the dharmakaya. The last point (non-abiding in the duality of samsara and nirvana) concerns the form bodies.

The Buddhas appear in the world but they are not identified with it. Through their great compassion, primordial wisdom, and other qualities, these self-arising ones manifest the ultimate stage of buddhahood, which is inconceivable even to a Bodhisattva of the highest (the tenth) initiation.[1]

---

[1] In this particular system of numbering the 10th initiation is the highest degree taken by a Bodhisattva before becoming a Buddha, and corresponds to the tenth bhumi.

Chapter 3

The Qualities of a Buddha

The Sixty-Four Essential Qualities of a Buddha

The dharmakaya (the unveiled Buddha-nature), and the (two) form vehicles (the sambhogakaya and the nirmanakaya) which are based upon it, are the cause of the liberation of one's self and others. They manifest as the 64 qualities of a Buddha.

The vehicle that embodies the highest truth (the dharmakaya) is of benefit to one's self. The (two) symbolic (form) vehicles of the wise are the basis for the best possible benefit to others.

The first (the dharmakaya), through which one attains liberation, is endowed with ten powerful superhuman faculties. The second (the two form vehicles), through which (sentient beings are guided), develops them so that they can attain the fruit (of enlightenment). It is endowed with all the qualities of the great ones.

The qualities of a (dharmakaya) Buddha are indivisible like space. His two form bodies are like the moon reflected in water.

The Ten Superhuman Faculties of a Buddha

The (ten) powerful, superhuman Buddha faculties spontaneously manifest like lightening (*vajra*), destroying the veils of ignorance. Like a lion they boldly act to remove the accumulated habit patterns of the mind (*samskaras*). 3/5

The ten powerful superhuman faculties are:

(1) Knowing the difference between natural and unnatural activity

(2) Understanding the effects of karma

(3) Knowing the essential nature of sentient beings

(4) Perceiving the awareness faculties of beings

(5) Perceiving their level of attainment on the path to the highest spiritual freedom

(6) Understanding of the full range of the path

(7) Knowing the difference between appropriate and inappropriate (practices) meditation and the rest

(8) Perceiving the past lives (of oneself and others)

(9) Clairvoyance

(10) Peace

(A Buddha) knows what is natural and unnatural. He knows the (cause and) effects (of karma). He understands the essential nature, the awareness faculties, and the station of beings. (He knows) the many aspects or stages of path (as well as) the appropriate and inappropriate practices (for each). He perceives the past lives through opened clairvoyant eyes. In this way the attained powerful faculties, manifest like a bolt of lightening, destroying the trees of psychic impurities and smashing the walls of ignorance.

The Four Skillful Means of a Buddha

There are four skillful means that are daringly executed.

By clearly perceiving the essential nature of phenomena, the (Buddhas) remove the hindrances (of the disciples) by teaching them the path (to liberation), thereby causing the cessation of their suffering.

By clearly perceiving the true nature of phenomena, and by causing others to perceive it as well, the Buddhas removes the hindrances to the path for themselves and others.

By teaching the path that leads to the attainment of the highest purity of awareness the Buddhas daringly bring about the cessation of suffering for themselves and others.

In the same way that the king of animals fearlessly deals with the other animals in the jungle, so the lion, who is the *King of Sages*, deals with the assembled obstructions (to spiritual freedom), with daring, independence, victory, and great skill. 3/10

Eighteen Indivisible Qualities of a Buddha.

The teacher manifests no hurried, idle, or incorrect speech, no loss of memory, no mental distractions, or conceptual divisions. Nor does he lack enlightened equanimity, pure or effortless striving, vigilance, or spiritual energy. His conceptual wisdom, which leads to spiritual freedom, is totally pure and unhindered. His non-conceptual wisdom, which is spiritual freedom itself, sees without impairment the essential nature of material and conceptual phenomena. His activity is motivated by, and is the manifestation of, this pure wisdom nature. The activity arising from primordial wisdom is totally natural. It is unimpeded in the three times (past, present, and future).

These eighteen qualities as well as the other (superhuman faculties and skills given above) constitute (the sixth vajrapada) the 'qualities of a Buddha.' They are not common to other beings.

The sage utters neither idle nor incorrect speech. His mind is not distracted nor does it suffer any loss. His view is balanced, undivided, and illuminated. He does not lack pure or effortless striving, spiritual energy, or vigilance.

Purified conceptual wisdom leads to spiritual freedom.

Non-conceptual wisdom *is* spiritual freedom. It is what perceives the essential nature of all things (material and mental).

The three activities of the Buddha (body, speech, and mind) are based upon this (doubly pure) awareness and so reflect it.

With this insight he boldly and with great skill turns the great wheel of the (Buddha)-dharma. 3/15

The Essential Qualities of a Buddha Cannot be classified as Phenomena

The phenomena of earth and the rest of the elements cannot be classified with space, which is without form, open, clear, unobstructed, and so on. Earth, water, fire, air, and ether all equally belong to this world. The pure qualities of a Buddha (like space) have nothing in common with the phenomena of this world.

The Thirty-Two Marks of a Buddha

The soles of his perfectly balanced feet are (each) marked with an eight-spoked wheel.

His feet are rather flat, with the ankles somewhat hidden.

A web connects his long fingers and toes.

His skin is as soft as that of a youth.

His body contains seven round protrusions.

His legs are like those of a deer.

His genitals withdraw into the body like an elephant.

His upper torso has the strength of a lion.

His shoulder blades are close together and high up on his torso.

His shoulders are well proportioned.

His hands and arms are soft, round, and well proportioned.

He has very long arms.

His immaculate body is surrounded by a mandala of radiant light.

He has forty, immaculate, pure, closely set, straight teeth of equal (number top and bottom).

His eyeteeth are very white.

His tongue is broad and long.

His refined sense of taste is supreme.

His voice arises from deep within and has an excellent sound like that of the Kalavinka bird.[1]

The foremost of beings has beautiful lotus-like blue eyes with thick eyelashes like those of a bull.

White hair adorns his face and between his eyebrows.

A mound-like protrusion crowns the top of his head.

His golden skin is pure and delicate.

His very fine bodily hair curls upward and to the right.

The hair on his head shines like a blue sapphire.

His well-proportioned stature resembles that of a nyagrodha tree.

The body of the great sage, which is incomparable and sublime, possesses all the power of Narayana.[2]

---

[1] Sparrow or Indian cuckoo.
[2] A divine incarnation.

The Buddha taught that these thirty-two splendid features mark (the body) of the Lord of Men. 3/25

Just as in autumn on a cloudless day the image of the moon can be seen reflected in a pond, so the disciples of a Buddha perceive the manifestations of the omnipresent as a reflection on the surface of the pond-like body of a Buddha.

The Sixty-four Qualities of a Buddha Explained

The sixty-four qualities of a Buddha, along with the basis for their attainment, follow the order as given in the (Buddha's) *Treasure Sutra*.[1] They have been described (above) as indestructible (faculties), bold (skills), indivisible (qualities), and symbolic (marks), and by such examples as a vajra, a lion, space, and the moon's reflection in the water (respectively). Of the (ten) superhuman faculties, the (first) six remove all the obstructions to clear perception; the (middle) three remove the obstructions to meditation, and the (last) one (that of peace) removes all remaining samskaras (subconscious habitual tendencies).

The (first six faculties) pierce the armor (of ignorance); the (next three faculties) break down the walls (meditative obstructions); and the (last faculty, that of complete peace) cuts down the trees (of the obstructing psychic impurities). 3/30 They are like a vajra for they are indestructible, essential, eternal, and unchanging. They are

---

[1] *Ratnasutra*

indestructible because they are fundamental. They are fundamental because they are eternal. They are eternal because they are unchanging. Because the sage is courageous, independent, steadfast, and victorious, he has been likened to a lion. He does not fear any of the assembled (obstructions). He is courageous because he knows directly the root source and cause of all things. He in independent (in his thinking) because he sees that others are not at his level of understanding. He is steadfast because his mind is steadily and calmly focused upon the fundamental nature. He is victorious for he has transcended all psychic conditioning.

Differences in Awareness

The differences in the awareness between worldly people, those who practice only for their own liberation, those who try to go it alone without a teacher, the wise ones (Bodhisattvas) or a Buddha, is subtle and very profound. 3/35 These (differences) have been likened to the five elements. The worldly (four) are like earth, water, fire, and wind. (A Buddha) is like the subtle ether of space, which is of the spiritual spheres, beyond this world.

The Dharmakaya and the Qualities of a Buddha

The dharmakaya, (the Buddha-nature totally unveiled), though indivisible like a rare jewel, has (for the sake of clarity) been divided into thirty-two facets of light, color, and form.[1] The thirty-two visible marks of the body (of a Buddha) that cause delight arise from the two form vehicles (of a Buddha), the illusory (physical) body and the subtle body. They are perceived in two ways. Those who are of the world and (therefore) far from purity perceive the physical body (of the Buddha) like seeing the moon reflected in water. Those who are within the mandala or sphere of the Buddha and are therefore close to purity, clairvoyantly perceive the subtle body (of the Buddha) like seeing the moon (directly) in the sky.

---

[1] These are the 32 qualities of a Buddha given above, the '10 indestructible faculties,' the '4 skills,' and the '18 indivisible qualities of a Buddha.'

Chapter 4

The Activity of a Buddha

The Activity of a Buddha Spontaneously Arises for the Benefit of Disciples

The all-pervasive ones spontaneously act for the benefit of the disciples according to their temperament, level of awareness, and training. This occurs at the right place and at the right time.

From the ocean of primordial wisdom arises a multitude of excellent qualities, which, like rays of the sun, continuously manifest through the vehicles (of a Buddha) as wisdom and virtuous activity. The great Buddhas of Compassion, like the wind, continuously blow away the cloud-like veils and impurities (that hide the Buddha-nature from view). They perceive that the essence of buddhahood is all-pervasive like space, without a middle or end, that it exists everywhere and in all beings and that it is the supreme treasure of virtuous activity. The compassionate activity of a Buddha is always spontaneous. This means that such questions as 'who is to be helped,' 'by what means are they to be helped,' and 'when and where are they to be helped,' do not arise.

The Cause and fruit of Spiritual Freedom

The cause and fruit of the liberation of those (disciples) with suitable vehicles is brought about through the elimination of all obscurations and psychic impurities. It is accomplished (by the noble ones) spontaneously and without premeditation. 4/5

'Liberation' means the attainment of the ten bhumis, the ten levels of illuminated awareness. The 'cause' (of spiritual freedom) is the two accumulations (wisdom and the merit). The 'fruit' is supreme enlightenment. 'Suitable vehicles' are those living beings that have accepted (the truth of) enlightenment. The 'obscurations' are the impurities, secondary impurities, and samskaras. The 'veils' are removed through continuous compassionate activity.

The six points have been compared to the ocean, the sun, space, a treasure, clouds, and the wind. The highest vehicle (the dharmakaya) is like the ocean for it contains the water of wisdom and the jewels of the (Buddha) qualities. The 'two accumulations' (wisdom and skillful activity) are like the sun vitalizing and sustaining all sentient beings. 'Enlightenment' is like space, vast without a middle or end. The essential nature of all living beings is the 'supreme treasure' for it is the same as the nature of the perfectly enlightened ones. The 'impurities' are like a multitude of clouds, unnatural, widely scattered, and unreal. The 'compassionate activity' (of a Buddha) is like a strong wind dispelling the (obscuring) clouds. The (compassionate) activity (of the noble ones) leads to the liberation of all living beings, whose nature is not different (from that of a Buddha). These activities continue for as long as the world remains.

Some More Parables

The (compassionate activity of) a Buddha has been likened to Indra, a drum of the gods, clouds, Brahma, the sun, a precious gem, an echo, space, and the earth.

Imagine that the surface of the earth is like that of a crystal ball in which can be seen the Chief of the Gods (Indra), along with a multitude of beautiful young goddesses, his magnificent palace, other gods with their palaces, all in glorious display. 4/15 Now suppose also that a multitude of people seeing this display were to develop the desire to become like the Chief of the Gods. And though this is only a vision, an illusion, it nevertheless has the power to greatly benefit the people for it may cause (some of) them to be reborn in the god realms.

In the same way if living beings were to put their trust in the vision-like appearance of a Buddha, endowed with all the visible marks and features, whose many benevolent acts, walking, standing, sitting, sleeping, preaching the dharma of peace, being silent, abiding in meditation, and showing various miracles and displaying great glory, and though ultimately an illusion, a thought-form, it nevertheless has the power to bring about the development of the desired conditions (for enlightenment).

And though ordinary people do not realize that this vision is merely a reflection in their own minds, the (illusory) appearance of a Buddha is nevertheless useful for the fulfillment of the goal. 4/25

Those who see this vision gradually develop themselves according to the (given) formulas. Soon they begin to see with the eyes of transcendental wisdom the vehicle of the highest truth (the dharmakaya) within themselves.

Now imagine that the surface of the earth is pure, clear, and transparent like a crystal ball and that within it can be seen Indra and the numerous abodes of the gods. Now imagine that its surface gradually looses its transparency and the vision is therefore lost. The multitude of men and women devoting themselves (to the images) offer flowers and such in the hopes of attaining (the god realm).

In the same way the Lord of Wisdom appears, like in a crystal ball, to the minds of the sons of a Buddha, who (then) direct their minds with joy toward supreme enlightenment. Like the appearance of the highest god's body in a crystal ball, so is the appearance of the body of the highest sage.

The appearance and disappearance of these images occur in one's mind. Whether the vision is pure (like with the appearance of the body of lord) or whether it is impure (like the appearance of the body of Indra in a crystal ball) they are nevertheless visions and (therefore) cannot be said to be either real or not real.[1] 4/30

Now suppose that due to the merit (we have accumulated) we are able to hear the continuous the beat of the cosmic drum. This cosmic vibration, which is sounded throughout the god realms, spontaneously, without premeditated action, effort, or physical form, invokes the slumbering gods to action. In the same way the Buddhas, spontaneously and continuously (without premeditation, etc.) teach in this world those with the necessary merit/karma the (Buddha) dharma of impermanence, suffering, selflessness, and peace.

In the same way that the sound of the cosmic drum is heard among the gods because of their karma, a Buddha's teaching is heard by those who have accumulated the necessary virtuous karma (merit). In the same way that the sound (of the cosmic drum) brings peace spontaneously without effort, premeditation, or physical form, so from the (Buddha) dharma arises the attainment of peace, spontaneously and without (effort, forethought, or visible form).

From the sound of the drum in the city of the gods arises the gift of fearlessness and the ability to destroy the army of the Asuras.[2] In the same way the teaching of the highest path, (which includes) single-pointed meditation on the formless nature, destroys the

---

[1] Longchenpa uses the analogy of seeing one's face in a mirror, it is a real reflection, but not a real face looking back. Thus the body of a Buddha is a real reflection of the Dharmakaya, but not a real body itself. This is true with all Phenomena.

[2] The enemy of gods and humans.

impurities and suffering of living beings, bringing unsurpassable peace. 4/35

The voice of the Buddha, because it (represents the) universal, because it brings benefit and bliss, and because it is endowed with a threefold miraculous power, is superior to the musical instruments of the heavens. Though the sounds of the drums of the heavens are great they do not usually reach the ears of those abiding on the earth. While on earth the sound of the drumbeat of Buddha's (teachings) can reach even those in the lowest sphere of samsara.

In the heaven worlds a great variety of musical instruments are used to kindle the flame of necessity. While (on earth) the voice of compassion sounds in order to extinguish the cause of the fire of suffering. Celestial music is sweet and is the cause of much elation. But the voice that the great Buddha speaks directs the mind toward meditation. In brief the voice (of the Buddhas) is the cause of bliss on many worlds. 4/40 In the same way that a person who is hard of hearing is unable to hear a soft voice, and (even) a person with clairaudient powers cannot hear all sounds, so the meaning of the very subtle teaching of the Buddha can only reach those minds that are free of impurities.

In the rainy season the clouds, naturally and spontaneously, drop water on the earth, thus causing an abundant harvest. In the same way the Buddha, naturally and without forethought, drops from the clouds of compassion the rain of the highest teaching, thus causing an abundant harvest of virtuous activity among human beings. In the same way that the rain when it descends is cool and sweet but when it reaches the earth takes on a variety of tastes, so the teachings of the Buddha descending from the clouds of compassion takes on the conditions and tastes of the people....

According to the five types of people, so there are five ways in which human beings pass through samsara, the continuous incarnations of death and rebirth. In the same way that excrement produces a continuous bad smell, so these people are in continuous pain. The great downpour of the sacred teachings from the clouds of compassion removes this suffering. 4/50

The wise ones know that searching for the objects of their desire through continuous incarnations is the cause of the suffering of gods and human beings. Therefore, they do not seek the glory of the gods or the ways of human beings.

By following with trust the teachings of the Buddha, by analyzing carefully, (saying to oneself) "this is suffering, this is its cause, this is the path, and this is its extinction," and through transcendental wisdom, suffering is perceived, its cause removed, the path is applied, and the extinction (of suffering) is attained.[1]

In the same way that Brahma, without moving from his palace manifests his appearance effortlessly throughout the god realms, so the Buddha, without moving from the dharmakaya, effortlessly

---

[1] This relates to the Four Novel Truths, 1) human beings are suffering, 2) the cause of their suffering is desire due to ignorance, 3) therefore, to remove the suffering one must remove the ignorance, 4) to remove the ignorance follow the eight fold Path.

manifests his appearance in all worlds to those with the necessary merit/karma....

In the same way that Brahma effortlessly manifests his image, so the Buddha manifests his form vehicles. 4/55 The Buddha descended to (his mother's) womb, was born, and lived a merry life in his father's palace. He then wandered in solitude, achieved victory over the evil one, attained supreme enlightenment, and taught the path which leads to the City of Peace. The Buddha manifested these events to the eyes of those with the necessary (awakened) qualities.

In the same way that the sun shines alike upon the lotus which opens its petals (to the sun) and the Kumuda flower which closes its petals (to the sun), so a sun-like Buddha (shines his light on world) regardless of the opened or the closed minds (of the people). In the same way that the sun acts naturally without forethought to bring the lotus flower to bloom with rays that shine everywhere, so the sun that is a Buddha shines the highest teaching upon the lotus flowers that are the disciples. The appearance of a Buddha arises from the sphere of enlightenment, the unchanging dharmakaya. His primordial wisdom nature, like the rays of the sun that shine everywhere, opens the (awareness) petals of the disciples.

Just as the sun in the sky shines upon the mountains, so a Buddha shines upon the disciples from spiritual space according to their virtuous karma. Just as the rising sun with its far-reaching beams gradually illuminates the world first upon the highest mountains, then the hills, then the valleys, so the sun that is the Buddha shines upon the assembly of beings according to their level (of attainment).

The sun does not reach everywhere on the land or in the sky. It does not have the power to illuminate the truth by dispelling the darkness of ignorance. (Only) the great compassionate nature (of a Buddha) can illuminate the darkness of ignorance with the many colored, all-pervading light rays of meaning and truth. 4/65

When a Buddha enters a city the blind are (often) given sight, which protects them from harm. In the same way those blinded by ignorance, who have fallen into the darkness of an external existence, are illuminated by the light of the sun that is a Buddha, so that their consciousness is awakened to the truth that before was hidden.

In the same way that a wish-fulfilling gem, spontaneously and without discrimination, simultaneously fulfills the wishes of each one according to their separate aims, so those who listen to the teachings of the Buddha spontaneously receive according to their thoughts and striving.

In the same way that the (wish-fulfilling) gem spontaneously produces the desired treasure, so the Lords always benefit others spontaneously, according to their virtuous karma, for as long as the world remains. 4/70

In the same way that a treasure hidden in the ground or in the ocean is hard to find, so it is hard for those whose karmic merit is small, who are held in the grip of their own impurities, to find the Sugata, the Unobstructed One, hidden within their own minds.

In the same way that the sound of the voice of another is heard, without thought or premeditated action, as abiding neither externally or internally, so the true voice of the Tathagata (Buddha) is perceived spontaneously, without forethought, as abiding neither externally or internally.

The (true) activity of a Buddha is like space—immaterial, invisible, and formless, without support or foundation (in the phenomena world). The (true) activity of a Buddha may seem, like the sky, to have high and low, (external and internal, etc.) but this is not the case.

In the same way that plants, when they grow in the earth, give no thought to the process, so the roots of virtuous activity growing in the ground of buddhahood do so naturally and spontaneously.

It is not generally considered that one could act spontaneously without premeditation, so in order to clear up any doubts of the disciples (on the subject) the (above) nine examples have been taught. Those who truly act for the sake of others, do so naturally and spontaneously, like Indra, like the cosmic drum, etc....

The activity of a Buddha can be seen in the purified, crystal ball-like consciousness of one with steadfast trust. The dharmakaya Buddha neither appears nor not appears. But according to the purity or impurity (of the minds of the disciples) so will the (two) vehicles of the Buddha appear or not appear as long as the world remains....

By following the example of the Buddha's enlightenment one enters the spiritual Path of virtuous activity, meditation, primordial awareness, and the total absorption in the essential nature of all beings and phenomena.

Chapter 5

The Benefit

The Last Four Spheres of the Buddhavajra

The Buddha-nature, enlightenment, the qualities of a Buddha, and the activity of a Buddha, are (all) beyond the concepts (implied by their names). Even those with pure awareness do not completely understand them. Only the leaders of the spiritual world understand them (completely). Those Bodhisattvas whose awareness is sufficient, who have trust in the vajrapadas, and who are possessed of the bodhichitta,[1] become pure receptacles for them.

If one who is striving to acquire the pure merit necessary to attain enlightenment were to make continuous offerings of land and jewels as numerous as the sands of the Buddha realms, it would not equal the pure virtuous karma generated from hearing and applying with openhearted trust just one word of the Buddha's Teachings. If one were to keep pure moral conduct for innumerable aeons it would not equal the pure merit generated from hearing, and applying with openhearted trust, but one word of the Buddha's teachings. If one

---

[1] The Bodhichitta is the pure natural impulse, originating from the Buddha-nature, to evolve spiritually. And while it cannot be created, it can be uncovered by removing the impurities.

were to perfect one's meditation to the point that one could enter (at will) the sphere of Brahma and could thus transcend the fires of the three worlds[1] (of samsara) it would not equal the benefit generated through hearing and applying of but one word of the Buddha's teachings.   5/5

Wealth arises from giving.

Excellent living conditions arise from virtuous activity.

Psychic impurities are removed through meditation.

Ignorance is removed through wisdom.

It is wisdom, attained through the application of the Buddha's teaching, which is supreme.

The four pure vajrapadas, as given above, consist of:

1) The basis (the Buddha-nature)

2) Its transformation (enlightenment)

3) Its manifestation as the qualities (of a Buddha)

4) Compassionate activity (of a Buddha) for the benefit of all

A Bodhisattva with heart felt trust in the existence, power, and benefit of these (four vajra treasures), swiftly attains the supreme awareness of a Tathagata. His heart felt trust arises from the awareness that the inconceivable, ever-present Buddha Essence 'exists within him,' and (that it has the 'power' to manifest as) the qualities and virtuous activity (of a Buddha). The bodhichitta, the

---

[1] The 'three worlds' are (1) kama-dhatu, the desire realm, (2) rupa-dhatu, the realm of the form producing conceptual mind, and (3) arupa-dhatu, the realm of the formless mind.

pure motivating impulse to achieve enlightenment, is thus realized and vigilant mindfulness, meditative stability, primordial wisdom, and the rest, are attained and not ever lost.   5/10

Because the bodhichitta is unchanging and eternal, the sons of the Buddha continuously move forward (on the path). In this way they attain the perfect purity and the highest merit. 'The highest merit' means that which arises from the five highest virtuous actions. Its 'attainment' means that the three aspects of activity (the giver, the act of giving, and the gift) are not perceived as separate. 'Perfect purity' means the total absence of all (mental and emotional) obstructions.

The Six Perfections

The (first) perfection of generosity is attained by giving.

The (second) perfection of moral discipline is attained through compassionate activity.

The (third and fifth) perfection of patience and meditative stability is attained through the practice of meditation.

They all arise from (the fourth perfection) of diligent effort and striving.

(These lead to the sixth perfection of wisdom).

The unity of Perceiver, Perceiving, and Perceived.

The primary cause of the veils of psychic impurities is the (false) belief that the three aspects of activity (the action itself, the one who acts, and that which is acted upon) are separate. The veils of psychic impurities are ('the five poisons') desire and the rest (hatred, anger, laziness, and distraction).[1] These veils are removed by supreme wisdom that is grounded in the study of the (Mahayana) teaching. This is very important!   5/15

Colophon

I have expounded this teaching for the purpose of attaining perfect purity for myself and to assist those with understanding, virtue and devotion. It is based solely upon the words of the Buddha and can therefore be trusted. In the same way that the eyes rely upon the light of a lamp, lightening, a jewel, the sun, or the moon to see, so this work is illuminated by the Teacher, whose words are brilliant with meaning, creativeness, and power.

Meaningful speech, the speech of the Master, is that which is in agreement with the (Buddha)-dharma. Unlike other speech it removes the impurities in the three worlds and shows the way to

---

[1] Desire prevents the perfection of giving, hatred prevents compassionate activity, anger prevents patience, laziness prevents applied diligent effort, and distractions prevent meditative stability.

109

peace. Whatever is taught in the light of the Victor's teaching by someone whose mind is not distracted, that makes the path to spiritual freedom attractive, should be placed upon one's head as the words of the Buddha.

In the entire world there is no one with more insight into the essential nature of things, more knowing of essential nature of reality, more skilled in the dharma, than the Blessed One. Therefore, do not distort the teaching of the great master for it would harm the Buddha's path! 5/20

Those blinded by prejudiced conceptions often find fault with the teachings of the great ones. Do not become attached to fixed conceptual views. Only a clean cloth can be dyed with pure color, a soiled cloth cannot.

The teachings given by the great arhats are not understood by those who lack intelligence, who lack faith in the virtuous doctrine, who indulge in pride, whose (essential) nature is obscured by neglect, who mistake relative meaning for non-relative meaning, who desire profit for themselves, who rely upon teachings opposed to the (Buddha)-dharma, who are repelled by those who follow the (Buddha)-dharma and who lack devotion.

The wise know that one should be more concerned of losing the profound teachings then the dangers of fire, poisonous snakes, murderers, or lightening. Fire, snakes, murderers, and lightening can only deprive us of a body, they cannot cause us to enter those terrible states of consciousness known as lower realms (avici). Even someone who has evil intentions towards the Buddha, who has killed his mother or father, or an Arhat, or who has caused disharmony or separation within the Sangha, their karma is quickly resolved through sincere contemplation on the nature of reality. This is not possible for anyone hostile to the dharma.

This ends my teaching on the seven vajrapadas—the Buddha, the Sangha, the (Buddha) Dharma, Dhatu (the seed of buddhahood within all beings), Enlightenment, the qualities of a Buddha, and the activities of a Buddha. 5/25

Through the merit that has been accumulated in this endeavor may all living beings see the exalted Amitayus of infinite life. May this pure vision awaken in them supreme enlightenment!

Book Three

The Middle Way

Madhyanta Vibhaga

Introduction to the Middle Way

Maitreya defines Emptiness, as 'non-dual reality.' To realize this reality, he tells us, we must tread the noble middle path that lies between and beyond the two extremes. The primary formula for understanding the non-duality of opposites was given by the Blessed One and reaffirmed by Maitreya in his teaching on the Buddha-nature.

> It is neither spirit nor matter.
> It is not both spirit and matter together.
> It is not other than spirit and matter.

This fundamental duality can be expressed in many ways—truth and illusion, being and non-being, nirvana and samsara, non-relative and relative, etc. The truth, says Maitreya, "is never one of two, one or the other, or even both together." "Emptiness," said the Blessed One, "has no opposite."[1]

> It is not a positive for it denies duality.
> It is not a negative for it affirms reality.

---

[1] *Parinirvana Sutra*

In this treatise on the Middle Path the fundamental duality that must be transcended is expressed in terms of mind—primordial awareness or Mind itself, on one hand and the conceptual rational mind on the other. "The mind," says Maitreya, "is both real and not real. Its primordial essential nature is real. Its appearance (in conceptual forms) is not. Reality is beyond both of these. This is the middle way."

In this teaching three primary aspects or levels of truth are explored:

1. The illusory appearance of conceptual and material phenomena
2. The Mind, which is the true nature and root cause of that appearance
3. The essential nature of reality (*tathata*), which is the integrated transcendence of both of these

"Mind," says Maitreya, "is the nature and cause of all things, beings, self, and the perception of the senses. Without the mind they do not exist."[1] The conceptual mind creates the forms, the illusion of appearances. It does not create the reality behind it. "The essential nature of awareness," says Maitreya, "is without any objects to observe. Equally, awareness lacks an observer." Longchenpa once said that primordial awareness is simply ordinary awareness, but without the clutter of concepts,

---

[1] *The Middle Way,* verse 1:3.

thoughts, attitudes, and emotions, without those aspects of the human psyche that are in constant change. When these ever-changing aggregates of the mind have been stilled through meditation, and the emotional nature has been purified through love, than that which remains is luminous clarity, non-dual selflessness and bliss.

The Teachings of Maitreya are the root source, through Asanga, Vasubandhu, and others, of the great Yogachara School of Buddhism. This school has been called *Chittamatra* or 'mind only' because of the above statement by Maitreya that is mind is the cause of all things. But this, as a name for the school, is misleading, for as Maitreya clearly states in the following treatise, the essential nature of reality is beyond the duality of the primordial mind, which is real, and its appearance as conceptual and material phenomena, which is not.

The Middle Way

Madhyanta Vibhaga

Chapter 1

The Nature of Emptiness

The illusion of appearances is caused by the mind's perception of duality.

Emptiness contains (the mind) and exists within it.[1]

(The mind) is neither real nor not real.

Its essential nature is real.

Its appearance is not.

Emptiness is beyond both of these.

This is the middle way.

The mind is the essential nature and cause of things, beings, self, and the perception of the senses. Without mind they do not exist.

False perception creates the illusion. But to say that nothing exists at all is false, because it has been affirmed (by the Buddha) that 'liberation is attained by removing illusion.' That which is

---

[1] This verse is similar to the famous statement made by the Buddha in the *Heart Sutra* of the *Perfection of Wisdom* 'Emptiness is not different from form and form is not different from emptiness'

perceived (the phenomenal universes) and that which perceives it and is its cause (the mind), are interdependent.   1.5

Reality is the unity and transcendence of subject and object (perceiver and perceived).

When this is realized the perception of an external world disappears. When this perception disappears, so does the perceiver. The essential nature of awareness is without any objects to observe. Equally, awareness lacks an observer.

In the three worlds[1] perception is of (both) the Mind itself and the (rational) mental faculties. Mind itself perceives the essential nature of an object. The mental faculties perceive its qualities. The first (Mind itself) is the fundamental basis of awareness (*pratyayavijnana*).[2] The second (the mental faculties) are those perceptions of mind (*manas*) that include the perception of the senses, thinking, feeling (emotion), and willing.

The world is afflicted by twelve great impediments (to liberation):[3]

---

[1] According to Vasubandhu the three worlds are: the desire realm (*kamaloka*), the lowest, next the form (*rupa*) realm of conceptual thinking, and the highest is the realm of formless (*arupa*) mind. The physical plane is not considered a part of the 'three worlds' in which we live.

[2] Pratyayavijnana is said to be synonymous with alayavijnana. Vasubandhu says that it is the basis of awareness (*vijnana*) because it is the origin of all the other faculties and perceptions of the mind.

[3] This translation of the twelve impediments along with the explanations given in parenthesis closely follow Vasubandhu's commentary.

1. By (the truth) being covered or hidden (by psychic impurities)

2. By past sowings (seeds of karma, *samskara*)

3. By being attracted (to bodies)

4. By predetermined or latent (tendencies)

5. By being completely absorbed (in the seven senses)

6. By the three-fold connection (awareness, the senses, and the object of the senses)

7. By encountering (pleasure and pain)

8. By (sexual) union

9. By being bound (by attachments)

10. By the fruition (of karma)

11. By suffering

12. (By the suffering of death and reincarnation)   1.10

These 12 impediments can be divided into a group of three (1, 8, & 9); a group of two (2 & 10); and a group of seven (3,4,5,6,7,11, & 12).[1]

Emptiness can be approached (from five perspectives).

1. Its essential nature

2. Its names

3. Its meanings

4. Its divisions

---

[1] Vasubandhu says that the first group contains the impediments of attachment, the second the impediments of past deeds, and the third group contains the obstructions that are due to present conditions.

5. Its proof

The essential nature of emptiness s not one of two—reality or illusion. It is not the same. Nor is it different,[1] It neither asserts nor denies.[2]

In brief, the names given to emptiness include:

1. Be-ness (*tathata*)[3]
2. The highest truth
3. Non-relative reality
4. The essential nature of phenomena
5. The Basis (of everything)

(The first) is unchanging.

(The second) is always true.

(The third) is the absence of duality.

(The forth) is the Bodhisattva's realization.

(The fifth) is the basis of the Buddha's power.   1.15

Emptiness is in the appearance of phenomena as well as in its unborn essential nature. The first is covered with stains and is not seen. The second I affirm to be like pure water, gold, or the

---

[1] Maitreya says: 'A distinction must be made between what is real and what is not, and yet (from a higher perspective) there is no difference between them at all." See *The Essential Nature of Phenomena* verse 10.

[2] Nagarjuna says: "To think 'it is' is eternalism. To think 'it is not' is nihilism. 'It is' and 'it is not;' the wise cling to neither."

[3] *Tathata*, though usually ambiguously translated as suchness, literally means the essential nature (ta) of being (tatha).

ether of space. The emptiness of the appearance of phenomena concerns the subject (the perceiver), and the object, his bodies[1] and environment.

Emptiness in its purity is (together) the awareness that perceives reality, the act of perceiving (reality), the (pure) motive for perceiving (reality), and the reality that is perceived. It is attained through a two-fold motivation:

1. To continuously help and not forsake the sentient beings in samsara

2. And for the attainment of eternal bliss

The Bodhisattvas are liberated by refining the innate Treasure Lineage (within themselves).[2] In this way they attain the purity, activity and qualities of a Buddha.

Emptiness pertains to phenomena, which is not pure, as well as to its essential nature, which is. 1.20 If phenomena was pure all beings would be liberated. And yet if there were no purity at all then liberation would be impossible.

---

[1]   Mental and well as physical.

[2] The Buddha's treasure lineage (*ratnagotra*) refers to the universal continuum of the Buddha-nature in all beings. To refine it is to remove the impurities that hide it from view.

Chapter 2

Obstacles to Realizing Emptiness

Obstacles to the two goals (the liberation of self and others), are very pervasive and limiting. (They arise from) excesses, conformity (to others), and from (an attachment to) abandoning (of afflictions).[1] There are nine kinds of obstacles:

Attachment to

(1) Excitement

(2) Equanimity

(3) Seeing reality

(4) Leading others to a view of self or in obstructing others in the attainment of selflessness

(5) This, (the truth of selflessness)

(6) External objects

(7) (The truth) of suffering

(8) The path

(9) The attitude of being satisfied with little

---

[1] Attachment to the practice itself is considered a subtle obstacle to attainment.

The obstacles that prevent the ten (*paramitas* or virtues), giving (and the rest) are different (from these). (They include):

A lack of will or resolve to eliminate the nonessentials

(A lack of resolve) to reframe from harmful activity

(A lack of resolve) to direct one's thoughts correctly

(A lack of resolve) to make the necessary preparations (to follow the Path)   2.5

A lack of potential

A lack of spiritual companions

Depression

Not practicing

Keeping negative and aggressive company

Negative habits

A lack of self-mastery

A lack of maturity in realizing the three (jewels)[1]

Negative karmic tendencies

Laziness

A lack of caution

Attachment to living (in a body)

Desire for pleasure

Dullness of thinking

Lack of confidence

---

[1] The Buddha-essence, the Buddha-sangha (the enlightened Bodhisattvas) and the Buddha-dharma (the Buddha's teachings).

A lack of faith (in the Buddha's teaching)

A lack of contemplation (of the Buddha's teaching)

A lack of reverence for the Buddha's teaching

Greed

A lack of compassion

Not remembering the teaching

Not applying the teaching in meditation

(The ten virtues which these obstacles prevent are)

1. *Subha*, giving (doing good)

2. *Bodhi*, enlightenment

3. *Samadana*, self-sacrifice

4. *Prajna*, wisdom

5. *Amoha*, knowledge

6. *Anavritta*, no need for rebirth (liberation)

7. *Parinati*, complete dedication to the Path

8. *Atrasa*, fearlessness

9. *Amatsarya*, without negative emotions

10. *Vasitva*, psychic powers

Each virtue removes three of the obstacles (given above).[1]

There are also obstacles to the 'wings of enlightenment' (meditation), the paramitas or ten perfections, and the bhumis (the ten stages of enlightenment). 2.10 (Obstacles) to meditation include

[1] See Vasubandhu's commentary on this verse for particulars. See pages 225-227 of *The Seven Works of Vasubandhu* translated by Stefan Anacker, Motilal Banarsidass, 2005.

sloth, lack of concentration, weakness, flawed instruction or view, and a susceptibility to distractions.

Obstacles to harmony and joy arise from not removing the obstacles to virtue (in oneself) and from forsaking the welfare, growth in the Buddha-dharma and happiness of sentient beings.

(Obstacles to) the (10) bhumis or levels of enlightenment include ignorance of:

(1) The all-inclusive goal (of the four highest)

(2) The (next) higher goal

(3) The (next) higher goal (after that)

(4) That which arises from it (which is the highest)　　2.15

(5) The goal of selflessness or non-grasping

(6) The divisions of the series (of bhumis)

(7) (The truth) that there is neither defects nor no defects

(8) The lack of diversity

(9) The fact that there exists neither inferior nor superior

(10) Ignorance of the four-fold potency

The antidotes to these ten obstacles are ten bhumis (themselves). Each of the obstructions is illuminated by a corresponding virtue or bhumi.

Chapter 3

The Fundamental Nature

(In this chapter the following will be examined:) The fundamental nature and its (three) characteristics, the true nature of cause and effect, the nature of ultimate (non-relative) and dense (relative) truth, the truth concerning of the nature of differentiation or diversity, the nature of spontaneous activity, and the truth concerning identity.

The fundamental nature (of reality) is three fold.

(1) It is completely unmanifested.

(2) It is partly manifested.

(3) It is neither manifested nor unmanifested.

The realization of this truth takes place when the dualities pertaining to phenomena or persons, subject and object, unmanifested and manifested, no longer arise. Reality is characterizes by the fact that it is neither manifested nor unmanifested. 2.5 (The 'partly manifested') is impermanent because is arises and then passes away. It is both pure and not pure.[1]

The fundamental nature (of beings) is selfless. It is empty of this (self) and that (the self of others). This pure selfless nature is not one's own (exclusively) nor is it separate from others.[2]

Suffering arises from a sense of separation. When this sense of (a separate) self ceases to arise; when the sense of duality (of self and others) ceases to arise, then the impurities (of perception) dissolve and there is peace.

With knowledge concerning the practice of removing the impurities comes an understanding of the truth of the path. This is designated as dense (or relative truth). 3.10

While the ultimate truth is one, it can be approached in three ways:

1) Practice

2) Attainment or realization

3) The fact (itself)[3]

The generally accepted understanding (of truth) lies with the first (or relative truth), while a true understanding lies in these three (practice, realization, and the fundamental truth itself).

---

[1] Its essential nature is pure. Its appearance is form is not.

[2] The 'pure selfless nature' is the Buddha-nature, our true identity.

[3] 'The fact itself' pertains to an absorption in reality that goes beyond realization. See Maitreya's *The Essential Nature of Phenomena* verse: 52. "The final perfection," says Maitreya, "is called, 'absorption into the essence,'"

While the truth is one it can, nevertheless, be expressed by signs and names (or relative truth), which differentiate it into two. Relative truth is dual. We are suffering because we have the habit of dualistic perception (perceiver and perceived). When perception become singular there is correct understanding.

The truth concerning progression (on the path) is two fold; adherence (to the path) and non (adherence), which causes suffering. The singular (non-dual approach) removes the characteristics of the (habitual) perceptions.   3.15

The self is (falsely) perceived (in the following ways):

As the doer

As the one who is the cause of bodily activity

As the one who experiences or perceives

As the one who possesses

As the one who is either bound or liberated

As the one who is afflicted or not afflicted

As the one who continues through time

As the one who meditates

(The antidote to these false perceptions of self are obtained by applying three types of skillful means)

1. A (conceptual) construction[1]

2. Discrimination[2]

---

[1] For example a step-by-step meditation practice.

[2] As in 'this is true, this is not true.'

3. (Realization of) the fundamental nature.

The first pertains to bringing together (in the mind) of several (conceptual forms). (The second is applied) through discrimination. The realization of the fundamental nature (lies in the understanding) that there is no (separation of) the perceiver, the perceived, and the act of perceiving.

The door that leads to unity (non-duality) is the (conceptual) experience and objective discrimination.[1] They are different (from the realization of the fundamental nature).

(The truth of) the cause and effect of all activity is, without question, (based upon) the interdependence or interconnectedness (of all things). Good or bad effects depend upon the following:

What is wanted or not wanted

Proper practice

Positive or negative states (of mind)

Attainment or realization

Behavior and control (of the mind)

Cause and effect is also affected by:

(One's) perception

By the continuity (of events)

(One's) experience

---

[1] Relative truth is the doorway to non-relative truth.

(An awareness of) the two kinds of purity (innate and
developed)

That which has already taken place

That which will take place.   3.20

(Skillful-means pertains to) understanding the feelings that are
the cause of suffering[1] and then applying the antidote.[2] Liberation
(form suffering and ignorance) arises (first) through discriminating
between good and bad qualities. (Then) through the realization of
the (non-dual) nature of self and others, which is wisdom that is
free of discrimination.[3] In this one must contemplate each aspect,
the preparation, the cause (of suffering) and its cessation.

---

[1] According to the Buddha's *Four Noble Truths* the cause of suffering is desire arising from
ignorance.

[2] The eight fold path.

[3] This is another example of first using conceptual wisdom to arrive at non-conceptual
wisdom.

Chapter 4

The Antidote to Suffering

To eliminate the cause of suffering, which is desire and ignorance, (as taught) in the *Four (Noble) Truths*, one must (first) contemplate and thoroughly understand the negative tendencies. (Then) one must approach and eliminate them through the development of a fourfold fiery striving in meditation.

The five negative tendencies (to meditation) include:

1. Laziness

2. Forgetting the focus (of concentration)

3. (The extremes of) dullness and excitement

4. Not applying the instructions

5. An (imbalanced) application the teachings

To remove them requires steadiness of purpose, clear focused attention and the development of eight qualities:

1. The basis (pure intention)

2. That which is based upon it (its application)

3. (Mindfulness of) the cause (the Buddha-nature)

4. (Mindfulness of) the result (enlightenment)

5. Not forgeting the focus of attention

6. Mindfulness (to avoid the extremes of) dullness and excitement

7. Vigorous effort to remove the negative tendencies

8. Natural or spontaneous tranquility   4.5

When the (meditation) qualities necessary to liberation have been developed, and one has attained mastery of (one's) intention and application, and the object of concentration is not forgotten, and wandering (thoughts) do not arise, then the negative tendencies are eliminated, and there is (clear) understanding and certain faculties, aspects and powers of enlightenment are acquired. (These include)

1. (Realization of) one's essential nature[1]

2. (Realization of the) basis or true (non-dual) nature (of phenomena).

3. Spiritual freedom

4. The (realization of) the benefit (to oneself and others)[2]

The three (highest) aspects are taught to be:

5. The foundation (of reality),

6. The state of (absorption with reality),

---

[1] The Buddha-nature.

[2] Earlier Maitreya stated that this 4th aspect of enlightenment pertains to the identification with the Buddha-nature in others or the realization the non-dual nature of self and others.

7. Be-ness (*tathata*).

The Path is eight fold:

1. Discriminating awareness (right view)

2. (Right) motivation.

3-5. The three aspects of good conduct (right speech, right action, and right livelihood)

6. Discipline or effort[1]

7 & 8. Mastery of the mind (concentration and meditation-*samadhi*)[2]   4.10

These are cultivated in three ways,[3] (from) without,[4] (from) within,[5] and through direct realization. For (average) people the (three aspect of good conduct), together with being satisfied with little,[6] eliminate primary and secondary adverse conditions and the obstacles to mastery. For Bodhisattvas concentration and meditation are superior.

(There are nine stages of entering the path)

1. The cause [7]

2. Entry

---

[1] The cultivation of the will.

[2] Samadhi is a state of profound meditative absorption where the separation of subject and object has been eliminated.

[3] depending on one's stage of development.

[4] Following the teachings or from the advise of the guru.

[5] Self-initiated effort.

[6] Non attachment.

[7] The Buddha-nature.

3. Preparation [1]

4. The result [2]

5. Effort

6. Without effort (unconditioned spontaneous activity) [3]

7. Understanding the distinction (between effort and effortlessness) [4]

8. The superior (realization)

9. The unsurpassable

These result in inspiration, realization, the power of spiritual activity and absorption.

The nature of phenomena can be classified (according to one's level of perception) in three ways, impure, neither pure not impure, and perfectly pure. Human beings can be similarly classified.

(First one) becomes a vessel (of the primordial wisdom nature). This is taught to be the ripening. From this one realizes power, joy, development, and purity. Through continual practice the favorable results that will eliminate adverse conditions will begin to develop. They will continue to increase (until) complete attainment.

---

[1] To cultivate pure motive, bodhichitta.

[2] A fully uncovered inherently pure bodhichitta.

[3] Effortlessness is the unconditioned spontaneous activity that arises from one's own inner spiritual -nature.

[4] Between the artificial and the natural.

Chapter 5

The Mahayana or Great Vehicle

The Mahayana is great because of its practice, its basis, and because it (leads to) full realization. Practice is six-fold (from 6 to 1).

1. Transcendent
2. Mastery of the mind[1]
3. The negation of phenomena
4. The negation of the two extremes
5. General
6. Specific

The practice becomes transcendent when it can include these twelve features:

1. Magnanimity
2. Persistence
3. Effort
4. Boundless (energy)

---

[1] In meditation.

5. Consistency

6. Effortlessness

7. Power

8. All encompassing (undivided)

9. (Responds to) the initiating impulse or cause[1]

10. Attainment

11. (The ability to) manifest (one's attainment for the sake of others)

12. Fulfillment

From these (practices) the ten perfections are generated:[2]

1. Generosity

2. Morality

3. Patience

4. Courage

5. Single pointed meditation (*samadhi*)

6. Intuitive wisdom (*prajna*)

7. Skillful means

8. Striving will

9. Power

10. Spiritual knowledge

---

[1] The Buddha Nature.

[2] The first six perfections lead to enlightenment. The last four give one the ability to benefit others.

Each of the ten perfections has an effect.

1. (From generosity arises) favoring others (more than self).

2. (From morality arises) harmlessness.

3. (From patience arise) tolerance-forgiveness.

4. (From courage arise) good progress.

5. (From samadhi arises) the refinement (of the consciousness).

6. (From insight arises) liberation.

7. (From skillful means comes) the ability to lead others to union (with reality).

8. (From the use of skillful means arises) power.

9. (From power comes) the ability (to bring others to liberation).

10. (From spiritual knowledge comes the means) to continuously ripen (others) to (the realization of) the joy (of liberation).

Bodhisattvas of the Mahayana path direct their minds (in meditation) toward the three goals:

1. (The realization of) the empty nature of phenomena

2. (The realization of) the original impulse (the Buddha-nature)

3. (The realization of) reality itself (*tathata*)

This is aided by ten dharma activities:

Imitating (the great Mahayana teachers)

Making offerings

Generous giving

Listening (to the teachings)

Putting the teachings into practice

Explaining (the teachings to others)

Studying (the teachings)

Reciting (the teachings)

Contemplating (the teachings)

Meditating

Due to the superiority (of the Mahayana teachings) this ten-fold activity brings about immeasurable merit (to oneself) and continuous benefit to others.   5.10

After the Teachings comes (meditation), (which involves) the removing the mental states of distractions and distortions.[1] To achieve an awakening of the consciousness in meditation the following must be removed:

1. Lack of will to hold the object of concentration.

2. The bliss (of meditation).

3. Mental excitement and dullness.

4. A sense of self (isolated identity).

---

[1] The mental distortions (*viparyasa*) referred to here are those that reverse true perceptions to their opposite.

5. Intentions.

6. Conceptual activity.

To be free of conceptual activity in meditation one must guard against:

The consciousness of name and form (*namarupa*)

The duality of the two characteristics of things

(Perceiving things as either) pure or impure

Fear and egotism

Name and form anchors the consciousness in the material. Dualistic appearances infuse the consciousness with conceptual phenomena. Purity and impurity refer to non-conceptual and conceptual perception. The essential nature of phenomena is pure while the appearance of phenomena (in form) is impure. Because these two do not exist independently they are inherently neither pure nor impure. The Reality is free of the two characteristics of duality, is (spirit) and is-not (matter).

This is full realization that is tranquil, without obstructions, distractions, or distortions. Though hard to comprehend this is the essential meaning of Middle Way between and beyond the two extremes.

www.ingramcontent.com/pod-product-compliance
Lightning Source LLC
Chambersburg PA
CBHW070719130626
46553CB00005B/2056